HOW TO INVEST FOR RETIREMENT

A SIMPLE PATH TO RETIRING RICH, INDEPENDENT, AND FREE

ANTHONY S. PARK

ISBN: 9781709902932

www.anthonyspark.com

Cover design by JD Smith Design

DEDICATION

For Mom and Dad

THANK YOU FOR YOUR FEEDBACK

Hearing directly from you, the reader, is the best way for me to make these books as useful as possible.

Please share how this book has helped you, or any suggestions for how I can make it better. You can email me at retire@anthonyspark.com or call me at 212-401-2990.

Thanks in advance for your feedback.

Best,

Anthony S. Park

CONTENTS

INTRODUCTION

If I could leave you with just two takeaways, they'd be:

1. Start investing *now*. Your greatest edge and power is time.
2. Winning at investing is actually very simple. Most information that says otherwise is selling you something.

WHO IS THIS BOOK FOR?

Keep reading if you're relatively debt-free, earning a good and growing income, and want to optimize every dollar you're saving.

My advice works better if you're younger, since I heavily emphasize compounding over time. But even if you're in your 40s, you probably have 20 years or so of compounding to work with before retirement.

A BRIEF OUTLINE

In Chapters 1 and 2, I'll review the basics; the time value of money; buy-and-hold investing; and the power of compounding.

Chapters 3 through 6 will explain why the only investment you need is index funds; debunk the common objections to index funds; clear up the overcomplicated notion of allocation; and discuss common investing mistakes.

In Chapters 7 and 8, you'll learn where and when to hold your index fund investments, and which accounts you should fill up first.

Chapter 9 will review your other retirement "investments," such as Social Security, pensions, and your home.

Lastly, in Chapter 10, I'll help you calculate how much money you'll need to retire.

Let's get started.

CHAPTER 1

PILLARS OF INVESTING FOR RETIREMENT

WHEN YOU'RE LOOKING FOR ADVICE ON SAVING FOR retirement, there's no lack of resources. Everyone even remotely connected to the financial industry is publishing his point of view. As we get deeper into this book, we'll examine a few of them—and point out the reasons why so much retirement "conventional wisdom" is actually anything but.

Most people giving financial advice see retirement from the wrong side of the field. They're on the front end, peering into the future and making assumptions. My point of view is a little different—and a lot more insightful.

As a professional executor for *hundreds* of estates, I see retirement on the back end, when the fruit of a person's retirement planning is laid bare. When you settle an estate, it's painfully clear when someone struggled to make ends meet late in life. As an executor, I see the checking and savings account balances, the unpaid bills, the neglected house, and the shocked faces of the heirs at settlement.

On the other hand, I've also seen the homes and finances of those who lived comfortably in retirement—the ones with clean balance sheets, a sizable cushion of cash in their IRAs, and well-maintained property.

Because I'm also an estate planning attorney, it's not hard for me to piece together the deceased's retirement plan (or lack thereof, in many cases). It's easy to see which financial decisions paid off over time and which approaches to retirement savings led to desperate times and destitution.

I often think that if some of these "financial advisors" had to manage the end result of their recommendations, they'd give different advice. I know my personal approach to my own retirement savings has changed because of my experience as an executor, and I've advised my friends and family members to re-examine their retirement plans in light of what I've learned.

SUCCESS IN RETIREMENT DOESN'T DEPEND ON YOUR INCOME

There's no great divide between blue collar and white collar workers when it comes to retirement planning. I've seen firemen, plumbers, and factory foremen retire far more comfortably than business executives, even though the executives earned a lot more during their working lives.

The difference is in the retirement plan. If you're well-invested (which you will be if you follow the advice in this book), you'll do better in retirement than higher earners who invested poorly. You can accumulate a sizable account balance with relatively small contributions if you have time and sound investments.

Norv was a self-employed electrician and never earned more than $100,000 a year during his working life. However, he made the maximum contribution to his SEP IRA every year and invested wisely. When he retired at 60, he had $2.2 million in his account, more than enough for a very comfortable retirement.

Nigel worked as a bankruptcy attorney at a medium-sized firm and earned at least $150,000 a year every year, and some years much more. He contributed the minimum amount to his employer 401(k) and put several thousand dollars in his IRA most years. Nigel fancied himself an expert in the stock market and took great pleasure studying the financial section to find the next hot stock. As a result, he was constantly buying and selling high-risk stocks and chasing market-beating returns. Unfortunately, many of his investments turned out to be duds. Despite contributing far more in real dollars than Norv, Nigel's IRA balance was just under $1 million when he turned 60.

DEFINING RETIREMENT

Before we go any further, I want to define the word "retirement" as I understand it so we're both on the same page.

Retirement is not having to work *unless you want to*. In other words, you have enough money to live comfortably through your natural life without pinching pennies. It's the exact opposite of a senior who is involuntarily unemployed and barely getting by.

According to the Census Bureau, 70% of seniors rely on Social Security to provide 50% or more of their income—and for about 45% of seniors, Social Security accounts for 90% or more of their income.

That is *not* retirement in my book. A person getting 90% of his income from Social Security is most definitely pinching pennies to scrape by. I've seen what that looks like firsthand because of my job, and trust me, you do not want to be one of the 45%.

TIME VALUE OF MONEY

An important concept in retirement planning is the time value of money, which is that money today is always better than money tomorrow. Even Popeye's friend Wimpy understood that: "I will gladly pay you Tuesday for a hamburger today." He may not have been a financial genius, but even Wimpy understood the time value of money.

Time works on money in two ways: compound growth (positive) and inflation (negative). All things being equal, $10,000 today is worth more than $10,000 five years from now, because in five years, that $10,000 would be worth about $15,000 if you invested it wisely, as I'll show you in later chapters.

Not only that, inflation eats away your money's purchasing power. If annual inflation is 3%, in five years, your $10,000 will buy goods and services that you could have bought for just $8,600 if you had spent the money today.

But you don't need me to tell you how inflation works. Twenty years ago, you could get a candy bar and a soda from the vending machine for about a dollar. Today, a Snickers and a Coke will set you back $5. That's inflation in a nutshell.

You should always take your money (or hamburger, if you're Wimpy) today, when you know its value and have more control over how you use and invest it. Not even top financial experts can predict with any certainty what the economy will look like in five or 10 years and what the tax rates will be. But you *do* know what $10,000 is worth *today* and its potential for growth if you put it in your retirement account.

BUY-AND-HOLD

If *time* is the most important principle for retirement planning, buy-and-hold is a close second. Throughout this book, I'll hammer that over and over, because it's one of the great equalizers between average investors (like me and you) and the Wall Street pros.

When you buy and hold your investments, you don't have to worry about timing the market because you're not trying to capture a few dollars in profit over a matter of days or weeks. You're going for long-term, exponential growth. When your time horizon is *decades,* daily market fluctuations shouldn't concern you at all.

Buy-and-hold eliminates unnecessary fees and transaction costs that suck money out of your retirement account. It also simplifies your accounting at tax time if you have money in taxable accounts. I'll show you in a future chapter just how much you lose by buying and selling stocks and fund shares in your retirement account—you'll be surprised how much even a little extra activity costs over time.

Finally, a buy-and-hold strategy frees you from the fear of periodic market ups and downs. If you look at the stock market over any particular six-month or one-year period, you'll no doubt see upswings and downswings, periods of rapid growth and minor corrections. But if you look at the market over a period of 10 or 20 years, the trend is reassuringly steady and upward.

Saving for retirement is a marathon, not a sprint. Buying and holding your investments is the best way to pace yourself for a solid finish.

AVOID SETTING YOURSELF UP FOR FAILURE

This might shock you, but if you follow the plan outlined in this book, your actual investment decisions are super easy. You literally do not have to think about them.

The hard part is avoiding all the pitfalls, drags on growth, and even outright scams that many novice investors unwittingly fall for. We'll talk about how to choose between two seemingly identical funds, where to look for hidden fees and expenses, and how to protect yourself against aggressive sales pitches for investments that seem too good to be true.

This information can make the difference between being well invested and poorly invested—between having enough to actually *retire* versus having enough to eke out a living for 10 or 20 years after you leave your job.

The thing is, you can fail at a lot of things over the course of your life. Most failures don't matter much in the grand scheme of things. But if you fail at saving for retirement, it will matter *a lot*. And you may not have time to recover from that failure.

A NOTE FOR THE MATH NERDS

Unless otherwise specified, the examples in this book are based on an 8% annual growth rate, compounded annually, which is the historical rate of return for the S&P 500. If you want to check my math—or run a few different scenarios on the examples I present—there are a lot of free online investment calculators and apps.

CHAPTER 2

COMPOUNDING: WHEN SHOULD I START SAVING FOR RETIREMENT? RIGHT NOW

ALBERT EINSTEIN SAID, "THE POWER OF COMPOUND interest is the most powerful force in the universe." If you're saving for retirement, that's true—but it's only half of the story. *Time* is the force that supercharges the power of compounding. That's why it's smart to start saving right now, even if you can only manage a small amount.

You can *retire a millionaire* saving just $500 a month for 10 years if you have enough *time*.

Imagine a new college graduate starting his first job at 22: if he invests $500 a month in an index fund until he turns 32 —and never puts another penny in his investment account— he'll have just over **$1,000,000** at age 62.

Compounding is the magic that turns that **$60,000** investment into **$1,000,000** with no effort at all on your part.

COMPOUNDING BASICS

Compounding is where your gains stack on top of themselves, and grow exponentially. Let's take some time to make sure everyone understands this building-block concept.

Step 1: How Investments Grow

The money you invest increases if your stock price increases. In some cases you earn dividends, which are profit payments corporations make to their shareholders. If you reinvest your dividends (that is, use that money to buy more shares instead of pocketing the cash), you'll generate more earnings along with your initial investment.

Example: Michelle decides to start planning ahead and buys $6,000 worth of an index fund in her IRA. The market goes up 6% for the year, so her IRA is now worth $6,360. How exciting!

Also, the companies within her index fund have paid dividends adding up to 2%, or $120. Instead of pocketing the $120, Michelle wisely decides to reinvest it into her index fund.

So now, after a year of growth and dividends, Michelle's investment has grown to $6,480. She's $480 richer without lifting a finger.

Now rinse and repeat for 30 years.

Over the past 50 years, the S&P 500 has averaged 8%

growth year over year. If you invest in an S&P 500 index fund and automatically reinvest your dividends, you get more shares, and those shares continue to increase in price and generate their own dividends, which are used to buy more shares...this process continues year after year for as long as you're invested in your fund.

So, if you open an IRA and make a $6,0000 maximum contribution to your index fund, assuming dividend payments are automatically reinvested for you, you'll have $6,480 in your account, or $480 more than your initial contribution, in just the first year.

Step 2: How Investments Stack, Exponentially

That's nice, you may say, but it's a long way from a millions bucks! Fair enough, I'll explain.

In year two, you're not only earning money on your original $6,000 contribution, you are *also* making money on that $480 in growth you earned last year. So, in year two you'll earn $518, not just $480.

Still not impressed? After 10 years, your investment is growing by $960 per year.

In my first example, if you've saved $500 per month for 10 years, by year 10 your investment will be growing on its own by almost $7,000 per year.

EARLIER IS BETTER...MUCH BETTER

Time is such a force multiplier that the person who saves a little money early in her working life comes out well ahead of the one who saves much more later on.

Let me say it another way: if you start early enough, you can save far less than someone who starts later and *still retire with a lot more money*.

Starting early: Emily opened an IRA with her very first paycheck and committed to saving $200 per month. She continued this habit for 20 years until age 42, when she left her advertising job to try her hand at freelancing and stopped her automatic contributions. When she retired 23 years later at age 65, her IRA was worth almost $700,000, even though she hadn't made another contribution.

Total contributions: $48,000

Retirement fund at 65 years old: **$700,000**

Starting late: Edward devoted his early working years to paying off student loan debt, buying a large family home, and funding 529 plans for his children's college educations. He opened his IRA at age 45, setting aside $1,000 a month for retirement. His IRA was worth just $593,000 when he turned 65.

Total contributions: $240,000

Retirement fund at 65 years old: **$593,000**

For the average investor, time is your *only* advantage when you're up against the Wall Street pros. They have better market information, and better research and analytical tools to go after big returns. They have trading technology that lets them time their trades to within a fraction of a second to capture the best price. They spend every minute of the trading day looking for opportunities to make a fast profit.

But when you have time to buy and *hold* your investments, the power of compounding gives you the edge, long-term. And as you'll see later on, not even the best Wall Street traders can beat the market consistently over time. Time is your secret weapon.

MAXIMIZING THE POTENTIAL OF COMPOUNDING

Compounding is a constant force working to grow your investment, but you can inadvertently sabotage its effects. New investors often fall into bad habits promoted by investment companies who are, let's be honest, always looking for ways to make money off *your* money.

If you want to get the best return on your retirement savings, you'll avoid these common pitfalls.

SKIP THE FINANCIAL ADVISOR

Many financial advisors charge a percentage of assets under management to handle your account. The average rate is about 1% of your portfolio per year. If you have $250,000 in your account, your financial advisor will take out a $2,500 annual fee to manage it for you.

Keep in mind, most financial advisors won't even accept you as a client unless you have $100,000 in assets—and some set the limit much higher.

You may be thinking 1% isn't very much, but over the long term, it can cost you a *huge* amount of money.

Example: Ajay wanted to get serious about retirement. He was glad to hear his old college pal Ramit was now a financial advisor. After a fun meeting spent mostly reminiscing, Ajay happily hired Ramit to manage his $100,000 IRA for the standard 1% annual management fee.

Ajay diligently contributed $500 a month for the next 30 years until his retirement.

Ajay's wife, Meena, started planning at the same time, but decided to put her $100,000 IRA into index funds without an advisor.

Miraculously, both Ajay and Meena's accounts performed identically, returning 8% per year over 30 years.

But by paying Ramit 1% off the top, Ajay already lowered his rate of return to just 7%.

So Meena's IRA, where she kept her full 8%, was worth $1,740,000 when she retired.

But Ajay's IRA, because he was paying his pal Ramit 1% off the top, was worth just $1,368,000 at retirement—**$372,000 less**.

Robo-advisors are a relatively new entry in the field of financial management. They rely on technology to replace much of the work of a live financial advisor—but they still charge you around 0.5% to manage your money.

Think it's a bargain? Let's look at the example above, but

say that instead of using a financial advisor at 1%, you pay a robo-advisor 0.5% to manage your investments.

Earning 7.5% over 30 years (8% average returns minus 0.5% to the robo-advisor), you would have $1,540,000 when you retired.

Robo-advisors = You just spent $200,000 for an app.

If you buy and hold the right investments (ideally index funds, more on that later), you really don't need professional advice to get better-than-professional results. When you step into retirement with almost **$400,000** less than you'd otherwise have, will you think your advisor fees were money well spent? Probably not.

PAY ATTENTION TO FUND EXPENSES

Mutual funds are extremely popular right now, and compared to buying individual stocks, they are generally much less risky if you choose well. But they come with their own set of fees that drag down your returns.

When you buy a mutual fund, the fund takes a percentage of the money in your account to pay the fund manager and administrative expenses. This percentage is called the expense ratio, and it ranges anywhere from 0.25% to 1% or more for funds with active managers.

Index funds tend to be the best value option overall in terms of holding costs; many have expense ratios of 0.02% or less

—or about 10 times less than the average mutual fund. The expense ratio affects the fund's returns, which can dramatically impact your investment over time.

Let's return to the example above—a $100,000 initial account balance and $500 monthly contributions for 30 years earning 8% a year. The table below shows your balance at retirement with different expense ratios:

Expense Ratio	Index fund 0.02%	Mutual fund 0.25%	Mutual fund 0.50%	Mutual fund 1%	Mutual fund 1.5%
Balance at Retirement	$1,732,000	$1,638,000	$1,540,000	$1,368,000	$1,213,000
What You Lost in Fees		-$94,000	-$192,000	-$364,000	-$519,000

AVOID ACTIVELY MANAGED FUNDS

Mutual funds are either passively or actively managed. In a passively managed fund, stocks are selected to replicate a market index or sector. The fund manager's job is simply to buy the same securities in the same ratio as the underlying benchmark.

Actively managed funds, on the other hand, hire a fund manager to pick and choose investments for the fund; the manager's stock-picking "expertise" is the main reason for the higher expense ratio. But actively managed funds cost you in other ways, as well.

Some mutual funds charge shareholder fees such as commissions when you buy and sell shares, and redemption or "market timing" fees if you sell shares before a certain period of time elapses.

Finally, turnover tends to be much higher in actively

managed funds. Turnover represents the number of holdings that are bought and sold within the fund. For example, if a fund buys Tesla shares and six months later decides Elon Musk is acting just a little too crazy for comfort, it might sell off all of its Tesla holdings and replace them with shares of General Electric.

Higher turnover means the fund is paying more fees to buy and sell stocks, and these aren't included in the expense ratio—these fees are *additional* money deducted straight from your retirement.

One study estimated that investors pay between 1.5% and 3.1% in transaction costs with actively managed funds. You already know that performance drag is going to cost you long-term.

Instead of hypotheticals, here's a real-world example using two actual funds, an index fund and an actively managed mutual fund. Both tracked the S&P 500. The performance data is taken directly from each fund's prospectus:

In 2014, Andrew opened an IRA with $100,000 and bought shares in the Fidelity 500 Index Fund with an expense ratio of 0.015% and a turnover rate of 4%. Five years later, his account balance was $168,770.

In 2014, Amelia bought $100,000 worth of JPMorgan Value Advantage Fund for her IRA, an actively managed mutual fund with a 1.14% expense ratio and a turnover rate of 161%. Five years later, her account balance was $153,900.

Both funds had similar actual returns before expenses. However, in just five years, Andrew made $15,000 *more* on his $100,000 investment simply by choosing a low-cost index fund instead of a more expensive mutual fund.

AVOID PAYING UNNECESSARY TAXES

If trading costs aren't enough of a performance drag, turnover transactions can also trigger a tax liability, further wrecking your returns.

If you make money on a trade—whether it's executed by you or your fund manager—the profit is taxed. If you hold the security for less than a year, the profit is considered ordinary income and taxed at the federal and state income tax rate.

If you hold the security a year or more, the profit is taxed as capital gains. Depending on your income level, you could pay as much as 20% in taxes to the IRS, and an additional percentage to the state if you live in one that taxes equity market gains.

There are two main ways to avoid tax drag:

- Buy and **hold** your shares—resist the temptation to trade. After all, if you're not selling shares and generating profits, there's nothing to tax.
- Keep your money in a tax-deferred account such as an IRA or 401(k)—even if you make money off trades, they won't be taxed.

There's a third way, tax-loss harvesting, but it's extremely complicated for most investors. Tax-loss harvesting involves selling off underperforming shares at a loss to offset any realized gains from other transactions. There are lots of IRS regulations surrounding tax-loss harvesting—make a mistake and you lose the potential tax advantage.

In addition, it's almost always a bad idea to sell off shares that are underperforming in the short term. The market is cyclical by nature. It goes through periodic corrections, but it always bounces back over time. Over the past 50 years, the S&P 500 has averaged returns of roughly 8% per year. If you hold your index fund shares for a decade or more, the law of averages takes care of your returns—you'll lose money long-term if you sell.

Even in tax-deferred accounts, buy-and-hold is still the best strategy. Though you won't pay taxes on your gains, you'll still pay trading fees or commissions on your transactions, driving down your overall returns.

NEED AN INCENTIVE TO START SAVING?

The first time you see the numbers proving the power of compounding, they seem unbelievable. It's hard to imagine how so little can become so much given time and compound earnings.

Try downloading an investment calculator app or bookmarking an investment calculator webpage and running a few different scenarios yourself. You can tweak your contributions, growth rate, and time to compound to see how it works in real life with your budget and time to retirement.

A bit nerdy? Maybe, but it's a great way to motivate yourself to save—and see how easy it is to dream big for retirement.

KEY TAKEAWAYS

- Saving a little each year when you're young yields better results than saving a lot when you're older.
- Expense ratios and transaction fees are the enemies of compound interest.
- Actively managed funds almost always underperform their passively managed counterparts.
- A buy-and-hold investment strategy is your best protection against taxes and fees that drive down your returns.

CHAPTER 3

WHERE SHOULD I INVEST FOR RETIREMENT? INDEX FUNDS, OF COURSE

ONE OF THE WORLD'S MOST FAMOUS—AND SUCCESSFUL—investors wrote the following instructions in his will for the money he left for his wife:

> *"My advice to the trustee could not be more simple: Put 10% of the cash in short-term government bonds and 90% in a very low-cost S&P 500 index fund. (I suggest Vanguard's.) I believe the trust's long-term results from this policy will be superior to those attained by most investors."*

The author of the will? Warren Buffett, the genius behind Berkshire-Hathaway, whose net worth is roughly $90 billion. When Warren talks, you should probably listen—at least when it comes to investing.

Buffett isn't the only billionaire boosting index fund investing. Dallas Mavericks owner Mark Cuban, currently of

Shark Tank fame, also recommends avoiding individual stocks and putting your money into S&P 500 index funds as a way "to own the whole market."

YOUR SLICE OF THE U.S. ECONOMY

There's really never been anything in the history of the world like the economic engine of the United States. In less than 100 years after the country's birth, it overtook the British Empire as the world's largest economy and never looked back. Our economy dominates every other country and it's not even close.

Warren Buffett tells the story of his very first stock purchase. The year was 1942, shortly after the Japanese bombed Pearl Harbor, and Buffett was 11 years old.

> *"I spent $114.75 on shares of stock. $114.75. If I put that $114 into the S&P 500 at that time and reinvested the dividends, think of a figure as to what it would be worth today. The answer is about $400,000. So if I as a little kid had taken that 114 bucks I'd saved— shoveling snow or whatever I'd done, I'd have $400,000 today. In one person's lifetime. That's America. I mean, that isn't me, it's the huge tailwind the American economy gives to any equity investor."*

Of course, Buffett couldn't have put his money in the S&P 500 in 1942, because index funds hadn't been invented yet. But *you can*—and why would you settle for 2% interest in a savings account or 1.5% in CDs when you could own your own slice of the American economy?

WHAT ARE INDEX FUNDS?

Index funds are an inexpensive way for you to "own the market," as Mark Cuban puts it.

In financial markets, an index is a way to track and measure performance in a particular market or market segment. There are actually about 5,000 different indices, but most people only pay attention to the larger, better known ones.

The S&P 500

The S&P 500 index tracks the performance of 500 of the country's largest companies by market capitalization. Because it reflects about 80% of the entire U.S. stock market, economists consider the S&P 500 a good snapshot of the U.S. economy as a whole.

The Dow-Jones Industrial Average

The Dow-Jones Industrial Average, usually just called the Dow, is the oldest and most widely used stock index in the world. It tracks the 30 largest U.S. corporations and represents about 25% of the entire domestic stock market.

The Nasdaq Composite Index

The Nasdaq tracks all the stocks traded on the Nasdaq exchange. It's the only exchange-based index; there is no New York Stock Exchange composite, for example. Tech companies are heavily represented on the Nasdaq compared to the other exchanges.

. . .

The Russell 3000

The Russell 3000 is considered a "total market" index because it tracks the 3,000 largest U.S. companies and represents roughly 98% of the domestic equity market. Because it includes 3,000 stocks, there are some mid-cap and small-cap companies in the index, but it is still driven by the largest companies.

———

So, indexes are hypothetical baskets of companies that serve as performance benchmarks; they don't own any stocks and you can't actually buy a "share" of the index.

That's where index *funds* come in. An index fund is a type of passively managed mutual fund that actually holds the same stocks in the same proportion as the benchmark index.

When you buy shares in an S&P 500 index fund, for example, you own a tiny piece of each of the 500 companies on the index.

Index funds don't try to beat the market, they simply try to *mimic* it.

Because there is no stock-picking expertise required of the fund manager, and very little turnover in holdings, index funds are usually extremely cheap to own—the largest and most popular S&P 500 index funds have expense ratios of 0.04% or less, or just $4 a year for every $10,000 invested. It's a viable investment model because these funds typically manage tens or even *hundreds* of billions of dollars.

This is where you should invest your 401(k), IRAs, and even long-term savings, as I'll discuss in later chapters.

WAIT, WHY SHOULDN'T I TRY TO BEAT THE MARKET?

Because investing in S&P 500 index funds already gives you a really good return on your investment over time without the risk and expense of picking individual stocks. Besides, it's virtually impossible to consistently beat the market over time, so why even try?

People get hung up on the fact that index funds don't try to *beat* the market—they only seek to *replicate* market performance. When you're dealing with the S&P 500, though, that is definitely not a bad thing.

Historically, the S&P 500 has delivered year-over-year average returns of roughly 10% over the last 100 years. Yes, there have been some extraordinarily bad years—the 36% crash in 2009 wasn't that long ago. But the market is now up over 300% since then.

Warren Buffett's bet

Remember Warren Buffett's belief that an S&P 500 index fund would outperform most active investors? In 2008, he decided to put it to the test, not against an *average* investor, but against Ted Seides of Protege Partners, one of the most successful hedge fund managers at the time. Buffett bet $1 million that the Vanguard S&P 500 Admiral

Fund (VFIAX) would outperform a basket of stocks picked by Protege Partners over a 10-year period.

Things started out badly for Buffett. The first year, the worst of the crash in 2009, saw his index fund lose 37%, while the hedge fund lost just 24%. For the next seven years, however, the index fund beat Seides's managed fund.

In 2015, the Vanguard index fund underperformed Seides's hedge fund for the first time since year one, though it was just by 0.3%. But in 2016, Buffett's index fund gained 12% compared to the hedge fund's 1%. When the bet concluded in 2018, the Vanguard index fund earned $854,000 overall compared to just $220,000 for Seides's Protege fund.

Did you catch that? **The "market" beat one of the best hedge fund manager's stock picks by 400%.**

Buffett's premise was proved correct, and Seides donated $1 million to an Omaha children's charity at Buffett's request.

Over the long term, it's not possible for even the best fund managers to beat the market. So why would an average investor even try?

WHY IT'S SO HARD TO BEAT THE MARKET

It's not impossible to beat the market in any given year, although fewer than half of professional fund managers accomplish it, as I'll explain later. But to truly "beat the market," you have to do it consistently, year over year, and that has historically been pretty much impossible.

Besides, "beating the market" means buying and selling stocks to capture a little more profit here and there. Every time you buy and sell, you're paying fees and potentially triggering capital gains or income tax to drag your returns down even more.

"I BEAT THE MARKET LAST YEAR"

In a single year, anyone can "win" against the market—and in fact, when a fund or financial advisor beats the market in a given year, they'll make sure it's splashed across all their ads and marketing materials. You may even have a friend or coworker who brags about beating the market with his genius stock pick.

But outperforming the market in a single year is not "beating the market." Seides, the fund manager in the Buffett bet, beat the market in two of the 10 years...but it didn't offset his poor performance in the other eight.

BUT CAN YOU DO IT CONSISTENTLY?

Beating the market only counts if you do it year after year, consistently.

Since 2003, Standard & Poor's has published a report each year known as the SPIVA (S&P Indices Versus Active) Scorecard, which compares the performance of S&P indices to the performance of actively managed funds benchmarked to those indices.

In 2018, actively managed funds hit a new record, although it's not one those fund managers should be pleased about. After 15 full years of historical data, 95% of active large-cap funds *underperformed* their benchmark index. Small-cap funds did even worse, with 97% trailing their benchmarks.

On a single-year basis, active funds do a bit better. Since the Scorecard started, between 40% and 85% of the active funds trailed their benchmarks, with the single-year average over the past 15 years hovering around 60%. If 60% of professional fund managers fail to beat the market in a given year, what do you think your chances might be?

Warren Buffett measures his own company, Berkshire Hathaway, by how it performs against the S&P 500 over a five-year period, not just a single year. He knows *anyone* can have one great year—but having five in a row is a much higher bar to clear.

HISTORY SAYS: NO, YOU WON'T

It should be obvious by now that it's impossible for anyone —even a Wall Street pro—to consistently beat the market, but some people point to Peter Lynch of the Magellan Fund as the exception that proves the rule.

Unicorn hunting? Peter Lynch managed the Magellan Fund from 1977 to 1990 and beat the S&P 500, occasionally by large margins, in all but two years.

This makes Lynch sound like a pretty remarkable

stock picker—and he was—but basic probability also explains his run of good luck.

There are about 9,000 mutual funds, and roughly 70% of them are actively managed. So each year, there are about 6,300 fund managers picking stock portfolios. SPIVA says that 60% of them in a given year, on average, do worse than the S&P 500, and 40% of them outperform. That's about 2,500 fund managers in a single year who beat the market.

The following year, 40% of that 2,500, or about 1,000, should outperform again, according to the statistics. In year three, 400 will outperform, the year after, 160 will, then 70, then 30, then 12, then five, then two, until finally, just one out of 6,300 will statistically outperform the market 10 years in a row.

Peter Lynch happened to be *that guy* in the 1980s. And no one's repeated his performance before or since.

What are the odds you'll find that one-in-6,300 fund manager who will squeak out marginally better returns year over year for 10 years?

FEES AND OTHER DRAGS

Besides the statistical impossibility of beating the market, trading fees and tax drag pulls down the performance of actively managed funds. The average actively managed fund has an expense ratio of 1.15%, or $115 for every

$10,000 under management. Compared to $4 or less for index funds, you're already way behind.

Then there are taxes and transaction fees. Actively managed funds have an average turnover rate of about 85%, with many funds having ratios as high as 400%. A high turnover rate means that the fund rarely holds stock for a full year; each time the fund sells off a stock, it's potentially a taxable event.

And remember, all those trading costs and transaction fees aren't included in the expense ratio—they come straight out of your retirement account. Taxes are also passed along to shareholders.

WHICH INDEX FUND SHOULD I BUY?

The short answer is the S&P 500 because it is *the* performance benchmark—even Warren Buffett's Berkshire Hathaway measures itself against the S&P. As do most actively managed mutual funds. If everyone is trying to beat the S&P 500, why not just go with the one they're trying (and failing) to beat?

There are about 3,000 index funds available in the U.S., pegged to every imaginable index. But when you look at lists of the top-performing, best-value funds, index funds pegged to the S&P 500 are always in the top 10.

The S&P 500 is diversified across 11 major market sectors. When you buy an S&P 500 index fund, you have exposure to all the sectors and industries in the U.S. economy. Companies on the index represent energy, communications, consumer staples, finance, healthcare, industrials, information technology, real estate, and utilities. In other words, if one sector is doing poorly, you're still insulated from bad performance by your exposure to the other 10 in the index.

SHOULDN'T I DIVERSIFY WITH INTERNATIONAL FUNDS?

You're already invested in the global market when you buy S&P 500 index funds—most of the companies on the index have a big international presence.

Some financial advisors might advise you to hedge your U.S. exposure with investments in international funds, but given the U.S. dollar's major role in the global financial system, weakening in the U.S. market would drag down other economies, too.

A U.S. financial crisis inevitably affects *all* global markets. But because of the resilience, relative freedom, and innovation in the U.S. economy, it tends to recover more quickly and with fewer long-term effects than other, more heavily regulated economies.

Why would you want to "diversify" by investing in countries that (a) depend on U.S. companies to drive economic growth, (b) have their currency pegged to the U.S. dollar, and (c) recognize the U.S. as their largest trading partner?

Diversify? Why should I? Since the U.S. economy is the greatest economic engine of all time, there's no logical reason to give up your slice of the U.S. market to bet on a foreign economy. Take a look at what you'd have in your account if you invested $10,000 for 10 years in index funds tracking foreign economies:

Europe — $20,002

The UK — $15,830

Brazil — $11,800

Japan — $21,609

South Korea — $19,600

China — $14,150

Southeast Asia — $23,607

Latin America — $12,680

S&P 500 — $34,950

Each of those economies had individual years where they might have "beaten" the U.S. economy, but none did so consistently—or by large enough margins to even come close to the S&P 500.

DOES IT MATTER WHICH S&P 500 INDEX FUND I BUY?

Probably not, as long as you have a passively managed index fund with a low expense ratio. You should never pay more than 0.10% for an index fund.

My advice? Go with a large, well-established index fund with a low expense ratio and billions of dollars in assets under management. Any of the following funds are solid choices, so pick the one you're most comfortable with.

If you already have an account with one of the firms, or your company's 401(k) is with one, you might find it easier to stay where you are. If you're opening a new account, check out each firm's website and app to see which one you like better.

Vanguard

Vanguard has an S&P 500 Index Fund that has $483 billion in assets under management, a turnover rate of 3.7%, and an expense ratio of 0.04%. Its 10-year average annual return was 13.69% as of June 2019. This fund is only available as Admiral Shares, so you need $3,000 to open an account.

Fidelity

The Fidelity Spartan S&P 500 Index Fund has $198 billion in assets under management, a turnover rate of 4%, and an expense ratio of 0.015%. It's currently the cheapest index fund tracking the S&P 500, and has averaged over 14% returns year-over-year for the 10-year period ending in June 2019.

Schwab

The Schwab S&P 500 Index Fund has $38 billion in assets under management, a 2% turnover rate, and an expense ratio of 0.02%. Its 10-year average return was 13.75% as of June 2019.

———

If you already have a brokerage account with TD Ameritrade, E*Trade, Ally Invest, or another online broker, you can buy Fidelity, Schwab, and Vanguard index funds through your existing account, but you may pay transaction fees. If you open an account with the investment management company itself, you typically don't pay trading fees on their index funds.

Finally, some actively managed funds have an index in the fund name, but aren't actually *index funds*. If you listen to certain financial talk-radio hosts, you may have been encouraged to buy some of these funds. If a financial "guru" is telling you to invest in a certain mutual fund, ask yourself what he's getting out of the deal.

Rule of thumb: Anyone telling you to invest in something other than an index fund probably has something to gain when you do.

KEY TAKEAWAYS

- Index funds give you broad and diverse exposure to the market at the lowest holding costs.
- It's impossible to beat the market consistently over time, so why waste money on active fund managers?
- The S&P 500 is the best snapshot of the U.S. market; it represents about 70% of the stock market.
- S&P 500 index funds are an all-purpose investment for long-term savings and retirement accounts.

CHAPTER 4

COMMON OBJECTIONS TO INVESTING IN INDEX FUNDS

OPINIONS ABOUT INVESTING ARE LIKE NOSES— everyone's got one and *most* of them smell. Opinions about index fund investing are no different. If you listen to financial talk radio or lurk on investing websites, there's always a group of naysayers offering negative hot takes on index funds.

Jack Bogle, the legendary founder of Vanguard Group, heard his share of hot takes when he introduced the first index fund in 1976. Leading financial experts at the time called them "un-American," "a sure path to mediocrity," and referred to the index fund as "Bogle's folly."

Today, about 70% of Vanguard's $5.1 trillion under management is invested in index funds. Unsurprisingly, Warren Buffett was one of Bogle's earliest cheerleaders. Buffett called Jack Bogle a hero and financial revolutionary.

"A lot of Wall Street is devoted to charging a lot for nothing. Bogle charged nothing and accomplished a huge amount" for American investors, Buffett once said.

That's something to keep in mind when you encounter some of the most common objections to mutual funds.

ALWAYS CHECK THEIR INCENTIVES

Most bad advice comes from people who make *their* money telling you what to do with *yours*. Remember the Buffett bet? In a recent letter to shareholders, Buffett wrote: "The majority of the wealth has typically flowed to managers who have promised their investors large rewards while delivering them nothing—or as in our bet—less than nothing of added value."

Many years ago, a woman visited her friend, who was a financial advisor in New York City. He took her on a stroll around the harbor to admire the yachts owned by the executives in his firm, the titans of Wall Street who'd grown rich on fees for financial advice. After about the 12th or 15th boat, the woman turned to her friend and said, "But where are the customers' yachts?"

Of course, there were none, because the real money-makers on Wall Street are the givers of advice, not the receivers. The advisory divisions of Morgan Stanley, JPMorgan Chase, and Bank of America Merrill Lynch took in over $40 billion in a single year. One study showed that around the world, the financial advice industry made $250 billion in fees to manage funds that failed to meet their benchmarks.

The "Where Are the Customers' Yachts?" line is actually the title of an excellent, humorous, and still relevant book by Fred Schwed Jr. Warren Buffett and Michael Bloomberg both recommend you read it.

When someone standing to profit from your money advises you against index funds, take it with a grain of salt. They know that the only one making money off index funds is *you,* and they'll be deprived of chipping away "their" chunk of *your* retirement savings.

SHOULDN'T I BE DOING SOMETHING?

In this case, *doing something* is simply padding your brokerage's profits. If you open an account with Vanguard, Fidelity, or Schwab, it costs you nothing to buy shares in their S&P 500 index funds—no commissions and no transaction fees. Your only cost is the expense ratio, which is as low as $1.50 a year for every $10,000 invested.

If you decide to pick and choose your stocks and mutual funds, you pay a commission or transaction fee every time you buy and sell, typically between $5 and $9 depending on the broker. Some mutual fund transaction fees are even higher. You could pay as much as 8.5% when you buy or sell your shares if you don't have a no-load fund.

Reza was sick and tired of hearing his coworker Hugh brag about how his latest stock picks were beating the market. Reza invested his retirement savings in a plain vanilla index fund offered through his 401(k), but he decided if Hugh could make money on the stock market, he could, too.

Reza discontinued his automatic 401(k) contributions and opened an IRA so he could pick and choose stocks. Every other Friday when he got paid, Reza couldn't wait to get home to pick three hot stocks to buy with his retirement savings.

Over the course of the year, Reza's IRA became an obsession. If one of his stocks had an off week, he unloaded it and replaced it with another. If a stock he owned was growing, albeit slowly, he'd dump it for one he thought would grow faster.

At the end of the year, Reza was shocked to see he had spent nearly $600 on trading fees, or 10% of his $6,000 annual contribution! Oh well, at least he could console himself by bragging about his amazing returns (before commissions) next time he ran into Hugh in the break room.

Except he was even denied that small reward: cumulatively, Reza's stock picks returned 6.9% compared to the 8% returned by his index fund.

If you're saving for your retirement, the very best thing you can do is to buy and hold low-cost index funds.

INDEXES HOLD LOSERS ALL THE WAY DOWN

People making this objection are almost always referring to the Enron collapse in 2001. The implication behind it is that a good fund manager would dump losing stocks quicker, and so outperform the S&P 500.

We know the data doesn't bear that out. Remember the SPIVA Scorecard? 95% of active fund managers failed to meet—let alone beat—the performance of the S&P 500 over the last 15 years, including of course down years.

Kevin and Natalie agreed to meet with Dwight, a financial advisor, as a favor to their insurance agent, who was a friend of Dwight's. Dwight's presentation promoting his firm's mutual funds was quite well done, but he could barely keep the smugness out of his voice when he pointed out that his company dumped Enron before it collapsed, avoided the Lehman Brothers fiasco entirely, and predicted the demise of Radio Shack long before it was dropped from the S&P 500.

Impressed, Kevin asked to see the fund's prospectus, expecting to find a history of superior returns. Dwight was pleased to point out the fund was ahead of the S&P 500 year-to-date, but when Natalie dug deeper into the three-, five-, and 10-year returns, they were nothing to be smug about, since they consistently trailed the S&P 500 by a significant margin.

YOU GET WHAT YOU PAY FOR

This is actually true, but not in the way the naysayers intend it. When you buy index funds, you are buying the brainchild of Jack Bogle, perhaps the most brilliant financial innovator of all time. You are also buying the business acumen and expertise of 500 of the most successful CEOs on the planet.

What do you get when you buy an actively managed fund? The "expertise" of one overpaid Wall Street stock-picker who *may* beat the S&P 500 one or two years over the course of his entire career if he's lucky—and charge you tens or even hundreds of thousands of dollars during your investing years for the privilege of losing you money.

Ingrid and Sam had a great relationship with Fiona, their financial advisor. Between their retirement accounts and the money Ingrid inherited when her father died, Fiona was trusted to manage nearly $2 million for them. She did a respectable job, averaging about 7.5% a year before her 1.5% management fee.

One day, Sam happened to catch an interview with Mark Cuban on Bloomberg where Cuban touted the benefits of S&P 500 index funds. Cuban seemed to suggest that Sam could manage his money without an advisor and get better results, an idea Sam found hard to believe.

That evening, he and Ingrid made a list of things Fiona had done for them over the years. In addition to managing their money, Fiona treated them to lavish dinners twice a year to go over their assets—usually at restaurants where reservations were hard to find. There were thoughtful Christmas gifts each year, and Fiona had given them tickets for courtside seats at a Knicks game. She even came through with tickets for *Hamilton* during opening week. It certainly seemed like they were getting good value from their relationship with Fiona.

Just to be sure, however, Sam decided to do the math. He realized that in the six years Fiona managed their money, they had paid her nearly $175,000 in fees. Not only that, Sam realized that he and Ingrid would have earned an additional $125,000 on their money had they invested in S&P 500 index funds.

So much for "free" Broadway tickets and dinners at Per Se.

INDEX FUNDS ARE NO BETTER THAN AVERAGE

If that's true, what does it say about the 95% of active fund managers who can't consistently beat "average?" Anyone who tells you a financial advisor or actively managed mutual fund will deliver consistent, above-average returns is either ignorant or lying. Warren Buffett's bet proved it.

People who say the S&P 500 is "average" are missing the big picture. The S&P 500 is the gold standard—if you were grading market returns on a curve, the S&P 500 gets an "A" and everything else is graded in relation to it. Funds that get

60% or 70% of the S&P 500 are the real "average," since that's how the vast majority of active fund managers perform.

Anything above the S&P 500 is the 100% plus extra credit, the A+.

INDEX FUNDS ARE TOO SAFE, YOU'RE MISSING OUT BY NOT TAKING RISKS

Not all index funds are safe; some are pegged to risky crypto or emerging markets indices. The S&P 500, however, is definitely one of the safest index funds you can invest in—and that's not a bad thing, especially for your retirement fund.

If you *do* feel the need to take more risks, and you're young enough that you can recover from one failed investment before you retire, go ahead and take a flyer. Invest 90% in an S&P 500 index fund and put the remaining 10% of your money into something with real upside potential, such as cryptocurrency or blockchain technology.

But *don't* put that 10% into an actively managed fund or speculative penny stock. You're not really diversifying or adding a new avenue for growth by choosing something that's already represented in an S&P 500 index fund.

Thomas wanted to goose the returns in his retirement account. He was happy with keeping 90% of his money in an S&P 500 index fund, but he didn't want to miss out on the chance to make extraordinary gains. After all, he still had 30 years until he retired.

At first, he thought about investing 10% in an emerging biotech or financial technology company. But after studying the companies on the S&P 500, he realized the best examples of both of those types of companies were already in the S&P 500, so he already owned a slice of the companies making those discoveries and innovations.

He finally decided to invest 10% of his money in a crypto hedge fund to see if he could get a piece of the next Bitcoin. If it didn't work out after three or four years, he would look for the next "big thing," knowing all the while, 90% of his money was making big gains off the S&P 500.

THERE ARE TOO MANY PEOPLE IN INDEX FUNDS; THEY'VE REACHED A TIPPING POINT

Index funds are all the rage right now—for good reason—and yet we've all seen our share of headlines predicting their imminent demise as a result of their popularity. The theory goes that once enough people discover a new investment or investment strategy, it loses its edge.

Here's the thing: index funds are hardly "new." Bogle invented them over 40 years ago, and people who invest in them see their advantages in the retirement account balances every year. It's only recently, when money is flowing into index funds faster than actively managed ones, that "smart" people are raising the alarm about them.

The reason is that incentives are stacked against index funds. Money managers—who have families to feed, children to educate, and lifestyles to maintain—know that index funds threaten their livelihood. That's why there is such a huge infrastructure supporting the financial advisor industry.

The financial industry knows how to prey on our psychology—their advisors are trained salesmen undergirded by sophisticated behavioral advertising and marketing campaigns, and rewarded by a fee structure that encourages referrals among financial professionals (see Kevin and Natalie, an all-too-common example).

Even if you and I see through the fog, most people won't. They will be persuaded by the advertising and marketing materials and get swept away by the promises of a financial advisor—because there are hundreds of billions of dollars in revenue depending on it.

KEY TAKEAWAYS

- Vanguard's Jack Bogle revolutionized investing for average Americans when he created index funds.
- Most people who object to index funds have no idea how the market works.
- Index funds will never reach a "tipping point" where they are no longer ideal vehicles for your retirement savings.

CHAPTER 5

ALLOCATION SCHMALLOCATION

IF YOU ASK 10 FINANCIAL "EXPERTS" WHAT IS THE most important decision an investor can make, nine of them will say asset allocation. Asset allocation is deciding what percentage of your retirement fund to invest in stocks, fixed income assets, and cash based on your risk tolerance and financial goals. Choosing the individual stocks and bonds is secondary to getting asset allocation right—or so most financial advisors say.

I'll show you why allocation is pretty simple, especially if you own a slice of the whole economy with index funds.

WHY DO FINANCIAL ADVISORS THINK ALLOCATION IS SO IMPORTANT?

The idea behind asset allocation is to help you reach your retirement goals with the lowest level of acceptable risk. Risk of what? You want to avoid the situation where if the market happens to be down when you need access to your money, you'd be forced to sell your stocks at a loss.

If you're saving for a down payment on a house, for example, you probably need your money in less than five years or so. You would have no time to recover if your investment lost money during that time. A financial advisor would recommend *allocating* all of your money into cash accounts or short-term bonds.

When you're saving for retirement, however, you have 20, 30, or even 40 years to let your money ride out the roller coaster ups and downs of the market, so you can afford to take more risks. When you're young, most financial advisors recommend a portfolio heavily weighted toward stocks with the balance in safe fixed-income assets like bonds to hedge against the risk of downturns in the stock market.

Henry saved aggressively for the down payment on his house, putting all his money in a stock growth fund. When his account balance hit $100,000, he was finally ready to buy a home. He found his dream house within a few weeks and made an offer. Unfortunately, the market suffered a major correction the previous week and was down 15%. Henry's stock account was now only worth $85,000. Not only did he have to sell some of his shares at a loss for the down payment, but he was forced to ask his father for money to close on his house.

Meanwhile, Henry also saved aggressively for retirement, putting 90% of his assets in an index fund. He also watched his balance dip 15% during the market correction, but he wasn't particularly worried about it since retirement was still 30 years away. He had no plans to touch that money, so he had plenty of time to wait for the market to rebound and the economy to work its magic on his 401(k) account.

WHAT ARE FIXED-INCOME ASSETS?

Similar to online savings accounts and other cash accounts that pay interest, fixed income assets are investments that pay a set amount to investors with much lower risk of losing your original savings.

Short-term bonds are the most common fixed-income asset, although certificates of deposit (CDs), treasury notes, and treasury bills are also considered fixed-income assets. Bonds are basically bits of debt sold by governments and corporations; they are considered "fixed income" because they pay out a predetermined amount on a fixed schedule. Think of them as a safe parking place for money when it's critical not to lose it.

The trade-off is that you will never earn as much on fixed-income investments—by a huge margin—as you will on an index fund. In fact, due to inflation, you actually lose purchasing power because bond interest rates rarely keep up with inflation.

Stocks down, bonds up? Some people buy fixed-income assets as a hedge against the market, believing if stocks are down, bonds will be up. But this isn't always the case. Sometimes they move in the same direction.

WHAT'S THE BEST ASSET ALLOCATION FOR RETIREMENT?

Warren Buffett disagrees with the recommendations of most financial advisors. Remember the instructions in his will? When Warren dies, he wants his wife's money to be invested 90% in S&P 500 index funds and 10% in short-term government bonds. That advice flies in the face of conventional wisdom about retirement savings.

Financial advisors stick to a rule of thumb that says you should have the same percentage as your current age invested in cash and fixed-income assets, and the rest invested in stocks. In other words, if you are 35 today, you should have a portfolio of 35% bonds/bond funds and 65% stocks/stock funds. At 70, your retirement should be 70% fixed-income and just 30% stocks on the theory that you don't want to risk your nest egg when you're counting on it for income, so it's best to park most of it in fixed-income.

I happen to agree with Warren Buffett: the best asset allocation at every stage of life is 90% S&P 500 index funds and 10% short-term government bonds—even *during your retirement*. After all, if it's good enough for Warren Buffett's wife, why isn't it good enough for you?

WAIT, ISN'T PUTTING 90% OF MY RETIREMENT IN THE STOCK MARKET REALLY RISKY?

The data says no. Let's just agree upfront that Astrid Menks (Buffett's wife) is probably going to have a *lot* more money in her investment account than you or I will, so she can afford to take more risks. But I don't think the Oracle of

Omaha would recommend the 90/10 strategy for his wife if he thought it was risky.

As it turns out, Buffett's advice isn't risky at all, even for average investors. Shortly after Buffett made waves with his will instructions, a study was done to test his assumptions. The study back-tested multiple portfolios—everything from 10% stock market and 90% bonds to 90% stocks and 10% cash (Buffett's recommendation).

The results were pretty shocking (and not in the way you might think). ***The worst-performing portfolio, with a failure rate of 13%, was 30% stocks and 70% bonds—the one most financial advisors recommend when you enter retirement.***

Buffett's recommended portfolio, 90% stocks and 10% cash, had a failure rate of just 2.3%, meaning just two out of every 100 retirees would not have a full 4% withdrawal in at least one year.

But the *truly* shocking news is that 98% of the people in Buffett's recommended 90/10 portfolio had more than twice the terminal wealth, or money in their account, at the end of 30 years compared to those invested in the "foolproof" 60/40 portfolio.

This means that retirees taking Buffett's advice could either have a much more affluent lifestyle with their 4% withdrawals, or they could leave a much larger inheritance to their children and grandchildren because their income needs are met with smaller withdrawals.

30/70 Example: Javier was always a stickler for

following his financial advisor's recommendations to the letter. When he retired at 70, he had $1,000,000 in his retirement account, 70% in a bond fund and 30% in an index fund. Each year, his advisor rebalanced the account, moving money from the index fund into the bond fund as Javier got older.

For 10 years, Javier took his annual withdrawals, but three days before his 82nd birthday, his financial advisor informed him he would only be able to take a full annual withdrawal one more year before his money ran out. He could either cut his withdrawals by half or two-thirds and hope to squeak out another year or two, or take his normal distribution and have nothing left the following year.

60/40 Example: Anna took her retirement planning into her own hands early on and decided on a mix of 60% stocks and 40% bonds for her 401(k), an asset mix she planned to keep throughout her retirement. She retired at 65 with $1,000,000 million in her account and a frugal budget based on $3,000 a month distributions.

Anna never emptied her account during her retirement, and when she died at 86, there was still $43,000 in her account for her heirs. Not bad, but kind of cutting it close...

90/10 Example: Carl invested 90% of his retirement savings in an S&P 500 index fund and 10% in short-term government bonds, just like Warren Buffett. When he retired at 59, he had

$1,000,000 in his IRA. Carl lived well in retirement, and actually increased his annual withdrawals by 5% each year. He even took an extra withdrawal every winter after he discovered the joys of senior singles' cruises.

Carl lived to the ripe old age of 90, and when he died, his children were shocked to discover there was still nearly $700,000 in his retirement account, given his wild spending late in life.

WAIT, WHAT HAPPENS IF THERE'S A DOWNTURN IN THE MARKET?

There *will* be downturns—that's what the 10% is for.

If you assume that you need 4% of your retirement nest egg each year to live on, and you have 10% of your assets in fixed-income or cash, you can raid your cash reserves during bear market years and avoid selling stocks at a loss—or even take cash dividends instead of reinvesting them. When the market recovers, rebalance your portfolio by selling off shares in your index fund to replenish your cash.

Historically, bear markets see an average loss of 30% and last about 13 months. Stock prices recover in an average of 22 months from the crash. There have been a few historical anomalies—it took nearly six years for the market to recover from the 2008 crash.

On the other hand, in December 2018, the market suffered its largest single-day loss *in history,* yet it was up 20% by May 2019.

Worst case scenario? You sell some index fund shares at a loss, but the majority of them remain in your account, generating higher returns and new wealth when the market recovers. Even with a downturn, you'll be in better shape than someone who kept 60% of his portfolio in bonds and lost out on the historical returns of the S&P 500.

Cora met her retirement goal of $1,000,000 when she left work at 65. It was a rough ride—she survived the dot-com bubble of the 90s, the crash of 2008, and the correction of 2018 with her IRA intact. Her money was invested 90% in a Vanguard S&P 500 index fund and 10% in a short-term government bond fund, and she felt good about her future prospects.

Unfortunately, she couldn't predict the Great Social Media Collapse of 2030, when the social media companies all crashed under their own weight and lost 70% of their combined value. By that time, the price of Apple products quadrupled, lowering the price of its stock by 50%. The market was in free-fall.

Cora's retirement fund lost $300,000 and she hesitated about cashing out index fund shares at a loss. So in 2026 and 2027, she switched off automatic dividend reinvestment and used her dividends for living expenses, supplementing them by selling off shares of her bond fund.

By 2033, the market had completely recovered and was slightly above pre-crash levels. To get her IRA back in balance, she sold off some excess index fund shares and bought more bond fund shares to replenish her fixed-income account, which had dropped to just 2% of her retirement savings during the crash.

WHY SHOULDN'T I JUST INVEST IN A TARGET-DATE FUND?

You could, as long as you don't mind losing out on hundreds of thousands of dollars. Target-date funds are a bare-bones type of robo-advisor without the bare-bones fees.

A target-date fund, or TDF, plugs you into a portfolio with an asset allocation based on your anticipated date of retirement—your "target date." These preset portfolios move your money from more aggressive and growth-oriented index funds to more conservative ones as you approach retirement.

By the time you retire, your portfolio is the absolute ***worst*** one for delivering reliable income in retirement (30/70), based on the study above.

But that's not all. Target-date funds are actually "funds of funds," which means that you not only pay the expense ratio and other fees to the TDF fund manager, you also pay the expense ratios for all the funds in your chosen portfolio. TDFs take a double-dip out of your retirement savings.

Vanguard and Fidelity do have some less expensive TDF options, at least in terms of fees. But they still cost you lots of money long-term since they stick with an asset allocation strategy that's been proven to fail. So why even mess with them?

KEY TAKEAWAYS

- Asset allocation has a major impact on your lifestyle in retirement.
- Conventional wisdom about how to allocate your money has been proven ineffective.
- The absolute worst portfolio allocation is the one most often recommended by financial advisors.
- If you leave 90% of your money in the S&P 500 even after you retire, you'll most likely be more affluent in retirement *and* have more to leave your heirs.

CHAPTER 6

DON'T RISK YOUR RETIREMENT SAVINGS ON THESE INDEX FUND ALTERNATIVES

Hopefully by this point, you're firmly in the index fund camp. You recognize they offer the best value for your retirement money and deliver the best returns over the long haul.

But maybe you caught one of the "financial guru" TV shows this morning discussing a too-good-to-be-true fund. Or you ran your retirement ideas by your dad, who couldn't believe you'd rely on yourself instead of a financial advisor for the most important money decision of your life.

Whatever it is, you're wavering and wondering if you shouldn't still consider other options.

Short answer: you shouldn't.

While nothing is *guaranteed* when it comes to the stock market, only one thing has 100 years of history you can use to guide your investing choices—the S&P 500. And index funds are the cheapest way of getting a piece of that growth.

WOULDN'T A FINANCIAL ADVISOR DO A BETTER JOB OF MANAGING MY RETIREMENT SAVINGS?

There's a certain appeal to having a financial advisor. You're wined and dined and may even be invited to VIP dinners at the rooftop executive dining room or in-demand restaurants. Let's face it, you feel like a big deal when you have a financial advisor doling out a few perks.

But as I've shown over and over again, financial advisors can't beat the market long-term, and they take huge fees out of your retirement account. There's really no reason to turn over your money to a financial advisor.

I don't want to bash the financial planning industry entirely, however. There are times when it makes sense to sit down with a professional and talk about your savings goals, tax strategies, and estate planning. As you gain more wealth, these check-ups can have value. That's when you make an appointment with a *fee-only* financial planner.

What's the difference? There are three ways financial advisors make money:

1. They take a cut of the money they manage for you.
2. They get commissions off the assets they buy for your account.
3. They charge an hourly rate or set fee for advice and consultations.

You *only* want to deal with advisors who get paid in the third way, to minimize the conflict of interest. Advisors who get paid a percentage or by trading your account will unconsciously nudge you toward solutions that will increase their fees. It's human nature!

Ask in advance what the hourly rate is or what they charge for a consultation, so there aren't any unpleasant surprises.

Even though fee-based advisors are cheaper *by far,* they sometimes *feel* more expensive because you're writing a check out of your household checking account. Management fees and commissions are just taken from your retirement account—money you don't even think about or notice, so you don't miss it.

But those fees add up to tens or hundreds of thousands of dollars. You might not notice it now, but you'll definitely notice it when you're ready to retire.

Fair-priced advice...: When Mitch and Allie got married, they met with a fee-only financial advisor to help them set up a budget and savings goals, and to talk through investment options. They paid $500 for the consultation and opened their IRAs with S&P 500 index funds. Every three years, they paid $500 for a "check-up" to make sure they were on track to reach their goals and tweak their contribution amounts for maximum tax advantage.

After 30 years, Mitch and Allie were exactly where they wanted to be for retirement, with $1.5 million in their account and a plan for timing withdrawals. They had spent just $5,000 in advisor fees to reassure themselves they had their finances in order and achieve an optimal outcome.

...vs. pricey wine and dine: Raymond and Hillary also met with a financial advisor when they got married. They were impressed with the advisor's long list of credentials, sleek office, and smooth, professional manner. They knew he was just the person to manage their money and set them up for an early retirement.

Over the course of 30 years, they met twice a year with Drake, their advisor, usually after he'd taken them out for an excellent dinner. Each December, they were invited to a VIP holiday party at the firm. Drake even gave each of their children lavish graduation gifts—almost like a rich and benevolent uncle.

When they met with Drake a year before they planned to retire, they were disappointed to learn that their retirement income would be 25% less than they needed it to be...and that Drake had taken over $400,000 in fees from their retirement account.

WHAT ABOUT MUTUAL FUNDS BENCHMARKED TO THE S&P 500?

An index fund *is* a mutual fund—the only difference is that the index fund manager simply buys and sells stock in the fund to mimic the composition of the index, while a mutual fund manager tries to pick stocks that will *beat* the S&P 500.

The index fund manager isn't trying to beat the market, he

is trying to BE the market. The mutual fund manager picks and chooses stocks and jiggers the fund composition in an attempt to outperform the index.

We already know that rarely ever works as a long-term strategy.

All that buying and selling triggers transaction fees and tax events that drag down performance—and that performance drag is in addition to the higher expense ratio of actively managed funds.

Actively managed mutual funds have an expense ratio of about 1% on average—which is 660% more than the 0.015% fee charged by the most efficient index funds.

One of life's greatest tragedies is that most employer 401(k) plans offer only mutual funds, which always have higher expense ratios than index funds. This is because it's expensive to administer a retirement plan—the regulatory compliance and paperwork issues consume hundreds of hours of staff time.

So employers outsource their entire retirement system to a financial services company that recoups its fees by offering their own mutual funds to employees investing in the plan.

The lack of quality, low-cost investment options is one reason I recommend reordering your retirement savings priorities—which I'll talk about in a future chapter.

A freelancer, free to choose index funds...: Eduardo was an independent journalist who worked on assignment. He managed his investments in his SEP-IRA. A Buffett acolyte early on, he put all his money into a Vanguard S&P 500 index fund with a 0.04% expense ratio.

For 30 years, Eduardo invested $800 a month. At 55, he had $1.2 million in his account and was contemplating early retirement. After traveling to exotic destinations for work, he decided it was time to revisit them for pleasure when he'd have the time to enjoy them.

...vs. corporate's forced 401(k) mutual funds: Emilia worked for a large employer who offered several mutual funds, one of which was benchmarked to the S&P 500, but had a 1% expense ratio. She, too, averaged contributions of $800 a month for 30 years, but between the expense ratio and the fund manager's inability to match the benchmark, her annual returns were 2% below the S&P 500.

At 55, Emilia had just $800,000 in her account and knew she would have to work at least seven or eight more years to reach her retirement savings target of $1.2 million. It was a bitter disappointment. Emilia had planned to hike to Machu Picchu as her retirement gift to herself, and at this rate, she feared she would be too old to tackle the Inca Trail and would have to settle for the seniors train.

WHAT ABOUT ETFS?

Exchange-traded funds, or ETFs, are very similar to index funds in that they are passively managed and pegged to an underlying index or commodity. But they're also very different. The whole point behind ETFs is the exchange-traded part—these funds are designed to be traded, just like stocks. Their prices fluctuate throughout the day based on what traders or investors are willing to pay for a share.

Index funds, on the other hand, trade like mutual funds. No matter when you place an order to buy or sell, it will be settled at the end of the trading day. The fund calculates the value of all the assets it holds and divides it by the number of outstanding shares to determine net asset value. NAV is what you pay for an index fund share.

Although ETFs have the same—or lower—expense ratios as index funds, you usually pay trading fees or commissions when you buy or sell them. If you buy or sell the index funds sponsored by your broker, you don't pay any trading fees. In other words, if you have an account with Vanguard and you buy Vanguard index funds, you won't be charged. If you trade ETFs, however, commissions and trading fees apply.

ETFs are better suited to active investors and traders who want to watch the market and time their trades according to price movements throughout the day.

If you are a buy-and-hold investor, which you should be if you're investing for retirement, index funds are a much better—and less expensive—option. It's just a matter of clicking "buy" and going about your business.

WON'T A HIGH-TECH ROBO-ADVISOR GET BETTER RETURNS?

Robo-advisors are the worst of both worlds. You pay fees just like you would with a human financial advisor, but you don't get any nice dinners or theater tickets.

Some people think you can't go wrong trusting your money to a robo-advisor algorithm because it's math! And science! And math and science and cutting-edge technology certainly has to beat the market.

Let's break down some robo-advisor myths.

ROBO-ADVISOR PORTFOLIOS ARE DESIGNED TO BEAT THE MARKET.

This isn't true. Robo-advisors design pre-set portfolios almost always built around ETFs. ETFs track an index, just like index funds—they replicate the performance of the underlying market.

The difference between the various portfolios is the percentage invested in different ETFs. You're paying a 0.5% management fee to have an algorithm choose how much money you should put in each index. You really don't need an algorithm to tell you where to put your money, since we've already discussed the wisdom of the S&P 500.

ROBO-ADVISORS REBALANCE MY PORTFOLIO SO I GET BETTER RETURNS.

It's true that robo-advisors frequently rebalance your portfolio—some even do it daily. What this means is that *every single day,* your robo-advisor buys and sells ETFs in your account so you're always in synch with your asset allocation strategy.

Unlike index funds, you pay transaction fees when you buy and sell ETFs. All that buying and selling to rebalance your account means more transaction fees taken from your retirement.

ROBO-ADVISORS ARE BETTER WHEN THERE ARE DOWNTURNS IN THE MARKET.

Some people think the robo-advisor algorithm will somehow be able to predict and adjust for market downturns. Since the first robo-advisor came online in 2009, there's really no way to prove it either way with data, since the market has delivered only positive returns since that time.

But logic suggests it isn't so, because robo-advisor portfolios are built around ETFs. They are only following the market, not leading or predicting it.

In the end, a person investing $1,000 a month with a robo-advisor for 30 years will have spent about $200,000 *for an app*. And you won't even get a Big Mac, let alone a fancy meal for your money.

KEY TAKEAWAYS

- If you must see a financial advisor, choose one who charges an hourly rate or set fee for consultations.
- Mutual funds rarely outperform index funds and can cost as much as 660% more in fees.

- ETFs are like index funds, but you pay transaction fees every time you buy or sell them—more money taken from your retirement account.
- Robo-advisors are the worst of both worlds—all the fees of a financial advisor and none of the perks.

CHAPTER 7

WHERE TO STASH YOUR RETIREMENT SAVINGS

Most of the time, choice is a great thing. You go to the store for fruit and you choose from apples, cherries, pears, even exotic kumquats and dragon fruit. It doesn't really matter what you choose, as long as it tastes good.

But when it comes to retirement savings, too many choices feels overwhelming. Planning your financial future isn't as simple as putting your spending money in a checking account, your vacation cash in a savings account, and your retirement savings in a retirement account.

Each different account type has advantages and disadvantages—and more importantly, different tax implications that can really impact your cash flow in retirement.

In this chapter, I'll cover the different types of accounts available for your retirement savings, in a big-picture way. In the next chapter, I'll get into the nitty-gritty of where to prioritize your savings so you get maximum growth and pay minimum taxes.

THE TAX-SHELTER OPTIONS

Everyone loves paying less income tax, which is why I'm covering tax-advantaged retirement accounts first.

A word about retirement accounts: you can open a tax-sheltered retirement account with an investment firm such as Fidelity or Vanguard—or even with an online broker like TD Ameritrade—but make sure you select *retirement* account for your account type. A regular brokerage account is a taxable account; there are no tax advantages.

I'll start with a simple chart like this for each account type:

Money in	Taxed or Not taxed?
Money grows	Not taxed
Money out	Taxed or Not taxed?
Required withdrawals	Yes or No?

Money in: Contributions into your retirement account can either be taxed or not taxed. If contributions aren't taxed, it means your employer puts them directly into your retirement account so it's not part of your taxable salary, or you put the money in yourself and deduct it from your taxes.

Money grows: Are earnings taxed or not taxed? All tax-shelter retirement accounts grow tax-free—you don't have to report the money you make from compounding while it's in a qualified retirement account, so you don't pay taxes on it. This is one of the huge advantages of a retirement account.

Money out: When you take money out in withdrawals or

distributions, it may or may not be taxed, depending on the type of retirement account and your age.

Charles had $1,000,000 in his IRA. He and his wife Zelda had paid off their condo in Hilton Head, sold their family home, and were ready to focus on their golf game. With Social Security and Zelda's teacher's pension, they only needed to withdraw $40,000 a year to maintain their lifestyle. Since Charles was 60, he could take regular distributions penalty-free and only pay his normal income tax rate on the money he withdrew.

Required withdrawals: There is one catch, however: unless you have a Roth IRA, you have to start taking minimum required withdrawals the year you turn 70-½, or forfeit *half* your required minimum distribution to the IRS. Sounds harsh, and it is, but the rule is there to keep the super-rich from finding another tax shelter to accumulate wealth indefinitely.

EARLY WITHDRAWALS

You should also be aware that the IRS will take a chunk of your money if you withdraw it from your retirement account before age 59-½, again, unless you have a Roth IRA. In addition to paying taxes at your current income tax rate, there's a 10% penalty on the amount you withdraw.

The IRS isn't totally heartless, however. If you have true

hardship—medical bills or disability, for example—they will waive the 10% penalty. But you still have to pay income tax.

Blaine had always planned to retire and travel the country in an RV someday. It seemed like fate when his uncle discovered he and his wife really didn't care for the RV lifestyle and offered Blaine their nearly-new travel trailer at an unbelievable price. Blaine found a good financing option, but he needed to put $35,000 down to get the interest rate he wanted.

Since the RV was for his retirement, Blaine rationalized withdrawing the down payment money from his IRA, even though he was only 55 years old. Because the $35,000 was treated as income on his tax return, and subject to the 10% penalty, he withdrew not only the $35,000, but a few thousand more to pay the income tax and penalty.

For each type of account, I'll give you the 2019 contribution limits, but these seem to change all the time, so make sure you Google current limits each year.

Let's get into each type of account.

DON'T TURN DOWN FREE MONEY FOR YOUR 401(K)

Your 401(k) is essentially an incentivized, employer-sponsored tax shelter, with a free money kicker. Today, about 80% of U.S. companies offer a 401(k) plan, and 100 million workers are invested in one. Americans have $5.7 trillion parked in employer-sponsored 401(k) plans. Here are the basics:

Money in	Not taxed (employer deducts from salary)
Money grows	Not taxed
Money out	Taxed
Required withdrawals	Yes

As of 2019, you can contribute a maximum of $19,000 per year in your 401(k) account, or $25,000 if you are age 50 or over.

What about the free money kicker? If your plan has an employer match—and just over 50% of companies do—you could actually save a lot more than $19,000 or $25,000. An employer match means that your company will invest one dollar for every dollar you invest in your account up to a certain percentage of your salary. The average employer match in 2019 was 3.5% of salary.

If you make $80,000 a year and worked for a company with a 3.5% match, your employer would match dollar-for-dollar the first $2,600 of your 401(k) contributions. In other words, you're getting a 100% return on your $2,600 right off the bat—which is why you should *always* contribute up to the limit of your company match.

Moira took a job at age 24 that paid $50,000 a year. It was a really terrible company, so she never got a raise for the entire 40 years she worked there.

But the company offered a 3.5% match for her 401(k) account, so Moira diligently invested 3.5% of her salary every single year in a low-cost S&P 500 index fund. Although she never got a raise, after 40 years, she had $1.6 million in her retirement account. In other words, her employer gave her $800,000 just for saving 3.5% of her salary.

EVERYONE NEEDS AN IRA—EVEN IF YOU HAVE A 401(K)

An IRA—individual retirement account—is an account you open yourself at a brokerage or financial institution. You control this account, not your employer, so you can choose where you want to invest. Unlike employer-sponsored plans where you can only choose among the funds offered by your employer's plan, you can buy *anything* with your IRA savings. You can choose to buy a Fidelity or Vanguard S&P 500 index fund for your IRA, or bonds, or even crypto hedge funds if that's where you want to put the 10% of your money you don't invest in index funds. It's totally up to you where you invest your money.

Here are the IRA basics:

Money in	Not taxed (deduction when you file)
Money grows	Not taxed
Money out	Taxed
Required withdrawals	Yes

You don't have to choose between a 401(k) plan or an IRA;

you can (and should) invest in both. Contributions to an IRA are limited by federal law. The limit went up in 2019 for the first time since 2013; it's currently $6,000 a year for people 50 and under. If you're over 50, you can stash $7,000 a year in your IRA.

Note—IRA contributions must be *earned* income. If you're a richie-rich living off a trust-fund, you can't take advantage of an IRA. This also applies to millennials who haven't left the nest and live off an allowance from Mom and Dad.

The good news is that IRAs are not based on a percentage of income. If you only earn $6,000 a year, you can still invest $6,000 in your IRA, and if you're the non-working spouse of a primary breadwinner, you can still contribute $6,000 a year to your IRA. This makes IRAs especially appealing for married couples where one spouse is the breadwinner and the other is a stay-at-home parent or only works part-time.

There is a catch, however. Although you're allowed to make contributions regardless of income, you may not be able to deduct them from your taxes if you earn too much. In 2019, couples with modified adjusted gross income over $123,000 cannot deduct IRA contributions if both partners have an employer retirement plan, or $203,000 if only one partner has an employer plan.

Savita was a doctor in a large hospital system earning $200,000; her husband Amit was an aspiring poet and stay-at-home dad for the couple's three children. Amit's income was sporadic; some years he earned a few thousand dollars from magazines that published his work, and others, he wasn't able to sell a single poem.

Fortunately, Savita's income was more than enough to cover the family's expenses, so the couple prioritized saving $6,000 a year in Amit's IRA whether he earned any income or not.

When Savita retired from her job after 30 years, Amit had $800,000 in his IRA. Because they avoided paying 35% income tax on Amit's IRA contributions over the years, the couple saved an additional $63,000 in taxes over the years.

ROTH IRA VS. TRADITIONAL IRA: WHAT'S THE DIFFERENCE?

Roth IRAs flip traditional IRAs on their head. You pay taxes *now* on the money you contribute, but you don't pay taxes on the money you take out. There are *no required minimum withdrawals* and you can continue to contribute to your Roth IRA right up until you die. You also aren't penalized for early withdrawals, since you already paid taxes on the money you put in.

Here are the basics:

Money in	Taxed now!
Money grows	Not taxed
Money out	Not taxed (...30 years later)
Required withdrawals	No!

It's a no-brainer for the IRS. They'll gladly take your tax money today in exchange for tax-free withdrawals 30 or 40 years from now.

This difference seems small, but it can have big consequences for your retirement savings. Most people are in the highest marginal tax bracket during their peak working years and in a lower one after they retire.

Tomas earned a great living as a petroleum engineer. When it came time to choose a vehicle for his retirement savings, he chose a Roth IRA because he felt he was in a much better position to pay his income tax now rather than in retirement when money might be a bit tighter. Over the course of his 30-year career, he paid 40% in federal and state income tax on the money he stashed in his Roth IRA.

When he retired, Tomas discovered his expenses were a fraction of what they'd been during his working years: his house was paid off, his children were educated, and he wasn't paying income tax on his large salary. As a result, his annual withdrawals were much less than his salary had been during his working years. Because of his lower income in retirement, his combined federal and state income tax rate dropped to just 27%.

Tomas actually lost money by investing in a Roth IRA. He paid 40% income tax on his IRA contributions when he could have paid just 27% on his withdrawals had he invested his money in a traditional IRA.

WHAT ARE MY OPTIONS IF I'M SELF-EMPLOYED?

Tax law goes out of its way to level the playing field for people who are self-employed and don't have the luxury of an employer match for their retirement savings. In fact, people who are self-employed may actually come out ahead in tax-free contributions compared to those who work for a company with a 3.5% employer match.

Dori is a self-employed tax preparer with no employees who generates $100,000 a year in profit. Dante is a security manager at a retail chain earning $100,000 a year from his employer.

Dori has a self-employed 401(k) and Dante has a company 401(k) with a 3.5% match.

If Dori contributes the allowable maximum to her retirement account, she can invest $39,000 a year (her own contribution of $19,000 plus 20% of her business profit, or $20,000).

If Dante contributes his 401(k) annual maximum of $19,000 and gets an employer match of 3.5% of his

$100,000 salary, or $3,500, he would only save $22,500 a year for retirement.

If you work for yourself, you have three tax-advantaged retirement options:

- Simplified Employee Pension IRA (SEP IRA)
- Savings Incentive Match Plan for Employees (SIMPLE IRA)
- Self-employed 401(k)

Money in	Not taxed
Money grows	Not taxed
Money out	Taxed
Required withdrawals	Yes

The basics are pretty much the same as 401(k)s and traditional IRAs. The difference between them boils down to your maximum yearly contributions.

With a **SEP IRA**, you can contribute the lesser of 20% of your profit for the year minus half your self-employment tax, or $56,000.

With a **SIMPLE IRA**, you can contribute $13,000 regardless of your self-employment income plus another 3% of your business profit.

If you have a **self-employed 401(k)**, you can contribute $19,000 plus 20% of your net earnings. You can also contribute an additional $6,000 a year if you are age 50 or over.

SHOULD I KEEP MY MONEY IN A SAVINGS ACCOUNT?

As you get close to retirement, you might want to transfer some of your money to cash, either in a branch or online savings account or short-term CDs. It's always good to have a small percentage of your retirement savings in liquid assets because it's money you can access whenever you need it. Cash never loses its value.

However, you should never keep the bulk of your retirement savings in low-interest accounts. Most savings accounts and certificates of deposit pay interest rates of 1% to 2%—returns that don't even keep up with inflation. You actually *lose* purchasing power when you put your money in a low-risk, low-return savings account.

You might get marginally higher rates with short-term bonds or CDs, but if you need your money before they mature, you'll pay a penalty for early withdrawal that wipes out even your tiny returns on these investments.

Savings accounts and short-term notes are great for money you need to access in a year or less, but everything else should go into your long-term retirement accounts.

DO I NEED A REGULAR BROKERAGE ACCOUNT?

Taxable brokerage accounts are useful for medium- to long-term savings if you've maxed out your tax-advantaged retirement accounts. A regular brokerage account is simply an investment account where you buy and sell stocks, bonds, and funds. Instead of earning next to nothing in interest-bearing checking and savings accounts, you have the potential to grow your money by investing in the market. There are no tax advantages to a brokerage account.

If you've fully funded all your tax-deferred accounts and still have money left over to save, you'll make a lot more in a brokerage account holding S&P 500 index funds than you would with an online savings account. Just know money invested in the market is always at risk compared to money sitting in your bank account.

OTHER OPTIONS FOR RETIREMENT SAVINGS

Your retirement savings won't just come from retirement and brokerage accounts. You're also putting away for retirement with your Social Security tax. The maximum monthly payment for the tax in 2019 is nearly $3,800. Benefits are pegged to your salary and age at retirement—you can't change your Social Security benefits by saving more or making smarter investments.

Although defined benefits plans, or pensions, are going the way of the dinosaur, some people will collect a pension check every month in retirement. Pensions guarantee an income every year regardless of your other retirement savings. In many cases, people who draw pensions also collect Social Security.

Annuities are insurance investments you can buy now to guarantee a certain income later—and we'll talk about them in a future chapter. We'll also talk about the role of home-ownership in your retirement savings plan.

KEY TAKEAWAYS

- There are huge tax advantages to saving your money in employer 401(k) plans and individual retirement accounts.
- Most employer 401(k) plans include an employer match—free money that really adds up over time.
- You can (and should) invest in both your employer 401(k) plan and your own IRA.
- Roth IRAs are good if you think you'll be in a higher tax bracket in retirement than you are today. Otherwise, keep your money in a traditional IRA.
- You don't lose out on tax-advantaged retirement savings if you're self-employed.

CHAPTER 8

PRIORITIES: WHERE SHOULD I SAVE MY MONEY FIRST?

It's not surprising if your head is spinning after reading the last chapter. There *are* a lot of account options for your retirement savings. This chapter is all about figuring out how to use them to your best advantage so you have the money you need when you're ready to retire.

Before we start, however, I need to point out that some of the accounts I'll discuss below have contribution limits and phaseouts based on income. I won't give you exact figures, because these limits change frequently. It's a good idea to check the IRS website each year to get the specific figures. You can also get the information from your CPA, tax preparation software, or free online calculators.

If you're after the best performance, your retirement savings priorities should look like this:

1. Get your free 401(k) money from your employer.
2. Max out your IRAs.
3. Top off your 401(k) up to annual limits.
4. Fund your emergency savings.

5. Put leftover savings in index funds in a regular brokerage account.

I'll explain my reasoning in a minute. But first—

NEVER, EVER SKIP A YEAR OF CONTRIBUTIONS

This is the golden rule of retirement savings, because you'll never get that year of contributions back. Retirement contributions aren't like cell phone minutes or data plans—they don't roll over year after year. If you don't contribute the max this year, you can't double up next year to make up for it.

Besides, you're not just missing out on *one year* of contributions, you're missing out on 20-30-40 years of compound growth. I've shown over and over in this book that time is your greatest asset in growing your retirement account. Skip just one year of $6,000 IRA contributions when you're 25, and you've lost $145,000 if you retire at age 65.

Once you skip a year, the opportunity to save and grow *that money* is gone.

Kareem always socked away enough money to get his employer match in his 401(k), but he wasn't as diligent about funding his IRA. He opened his account on his 30th birthday and funded it fully for a couple of years, but then his first child arrived, and he missed a couple of years—babies are expensive!

Over the next 30 years, Kareem was hit-and-miss

with his IRA. Each time a new child came, he missed a year or two. When his wife switched to part-time work, he missed another few years. He didn't make any contributions at all when his children were in college.

By the time Kareem retired, he had only fully funded his IRA 21 out of 35 years. When he retired at 65, his IRA had $750,000 in it. Had he funded it the entire 35 years, he would have had $1.125 million. By skipping $84,000 in contributions over the years, he lost nearly $300,000 in retirement savings growth.

STEP ONE: MAX OUT YOUR FREE 401(K) MONEY

This one is a no-brainer. If you get matching contributions from your employer, max them out.

Chances are good your company has an employer match program; about 75% of U.S. businesses do. The average matching contribution is nearly 5%, which means you're getting *at least* a 100% return on 5% of your salary if you stash it in your 401(k).

Your employer may have a different match, but whatever it is, make sure you take full advantage of it. Why leave free money on the table? In the last chapter, you saw how just 3.5% of a $50,000 salary added up to $800,000 in retirement.

The downside with employer-sponsored plans is that often —though not always—the fund choices are less than ideal. Depending on the plan, you may have a selection of target date funds and actively managed funds, none of which keep pace with the S&P 500 and cost two to three times as much to own.

Carlton's company matches up to 6% of his $100,000 salary in 401(k) contributions each year. Carlton contributes $6,000 and gets the full $6,000 match (free money) from his employer. He invests the money in his plan's large-cap growth fund, which comes close to S&P 500 returns and has a 1% expense ratio.

Carrie's company only matches 5% of her $100,000 salary, but offers an S&P 500 index fund with an expense ratio of 0.05%. She also contributes 5% each year to take full advantage of her matching funds.

When Carlton retires after 30 years of $6,000 annual contributions, plus an additional $6,000 a year in free money, his 401(k) will have a balance of $1.1 million.

When Carrie retires after 30 years of $5,000 annual contributions plus free money, her 401(k) will have a balance of $1.25 million. She will contribute less but end up with $150,000 more because she has better fund options.

If you're Carrie and you have a low-cost index fund option in your company plan, your retirement priorities are simple.

You max out your 401(k) contributions up to the annual limit and move on to other savings priorities.

If you're Carlton, on the other hand, and your fund choices aren't that great, you stop at 6% (or whatever your employer match is) for your 401(k) and move on to Step Two.

STEP TWO: MAX OUT YOUR TRADITIONAL OR ROTH IRA

I know what you're thinking: Why would I bother with *another* account when I could just up my contribution to my employer 401(k)?

And here's my answer: Why *wouldn't* you spend 10 minutes to open and fund another account if you're getting an extra 1% to 2% a year in returns? You already know from previous chapters that a difference of even 0.5% can add up to hundreds of thousands of dollars when you have 30 years of compound growth.

It's fine to accept subpar returns on your retirement savings when you're getting a 100% company match—no amount of compounding replaces that free money.

But on your unmatched contributions, you look for every advantage, and that means the lowest-cost funds with the best long-term performance.

If it helps you to simplify and work with just one broker, one username and one password, you can open your IRA with the same company that administers your 401(k), if it offers low-cost index funds. For example, if Charles Schwab provides your company 401(k), open a Schwab IRA. If that's not an option, go with Vanguard, Fidelity, or an online brokerage.

TRADITIONAL OR ROTH IRA?

The simple answer is always traditional—but as you've probably figured out, retirement savings are rarely simple. Anyone who earns income and is under age 70-½ can contribute to a traditional IRA, but you lose the tax deduction once you hit a certain income level. The phaseout level is based on income and whether or not you're covered by a 401(k) or other workplace retirement plan.

Once you phase out of the IRA tax deduction, then you contribute to a Roth IRA.

I know a lot of advisors push Roth IRAs, but that doesn't make sense. Remember, you pay income tax on your contributions today and withdraw the money tax-free in retirement. That sounds like a good idea, but as you saw in the previous chapter, it's rarely the smartest move. Remember Wimpy?

Most people are in peak earning years when they max out their IRA contributions—the years when they're in the highest tax bracket. You'll probably live on much less in retirement than you will right now when you're paying a large mortgage, raising kids, and funding college educations. And when you're drawing less income, you're in a lower tax bracket.

So why pay higher taxes on the money now when you could pay lower taxes on it later?

If you qualify for a traditional IRA, you only have to earn $5,000 to put $5,000 in your IRA. If you're in the top federal tax bracket and you live in a state that collects income tax, you'll need to earn about $6,500 to contribute $5,000 to a Roth IRA.

Danya pays 30% in combined federal and state income tax. Based on her salary of $100,000, she plans to contribute $6,000 to her Roth IRA. However, since Roth contributions are made with after-tax dollars, her $6,000 contribution actually eats up $7,800 of her salary given her 30% income tax burden.

For most people, taking the tax deduction now and paying taxes in retirement is clearly a win. Based on today's tax tables, a married couple would need to withdraw about $600,000 a year to hit the top tax bracket. It's unlikely your required minimum distributions will ever hit that level—and if they do, I would say your financial situation in retirement is pretty secure. Hitting the top tax bracket in retirement is not exactly a bad problem to have.

Now, there *are* situations where a Roth IRA makes sense over a traditional IRA. If you're working part-time or have an entry-level job and pay nothing or next-to-nothing in income tax, go ahead and put your retirement savings in a Roth IRA. And if you live in a state that doesn't collect income tax, the tax deduction may not have as much of an impact. Finally, if your income disqualifies you for a traditional IRA tax deduction but you can still contribute to a Roth, there's no reason not to do so.

Kim lived with his parents and worked part-time as a teaching assistant for four years while he finished his PhD. He earned about $10,000 a year, which put him in the lowest tax bracket. He opted to contribute to a Roth IRA during those years, because he anticipated being in a higher tax bracket when he retired.

STEP THREE: TOP OFF YOUR 401(K) ACCOUNT

If you maxed out your contributions in step one because you have great index fund choices, this step doesn't apply to you.

On the other hand, if you still have money to save after your matched 401(k) contributions and your IRA contributions, use it to max out your employer 401(k) with pre-tax dollars.

A word of caution, however: if your fund choices are *really bad,* you might want to skip this and move on to the next step.

Kelly was excited to start her new job with an architectural firm. She was even more pleased to learn the company offered 100% matching up to 8% of her salary. The wind went out of her sails when she saw her investment options: her company only offered target-date funds. Kelly was 45, which meant that almost half of her retirement savings would be tied up in low-yield bond funds. To make matters worse, the plan administrator charged nearly 2% to manage the fund. Kelly contributed the full 8% to get the company match, maxed out her IRA, and put the rest of her savings in index funds in a brokerage account.

STEP FOUR: FUND YOUR EMERGENCY SAVINGS

In some financial circles, this advice amounts to heresy—most advisors will tell you an emergency fund should be your first priority. But bear with me, because putting your money into your 401(k) and IRA first actually makes *better* financial sense.

First, let's define an emergency fund. This money is your safety net—it keeps you going in the event you lose your job or have a serious illness or injury. It's also there when you have major home repairs not covered by insurance, like replacing a leaky roof or broken HVAC unit. It's not your vacation money or buy-a-new-car money.

A good rule of thumb is to have six months of expenses tucked away in liquid savings like an interest-bearing checking or savings account. In other words, if you need $5,000 a month to pay your mortgage, car payments, utilities, insurance, and food, you need $30,000 in your emergency account. But you don't have to go overboard, especially in a two-income family; you may be fine with just three months in your emergency account.

You shouldn't keep emergency funds in bonds or CDs because you pay a penalty if you need the money before they mature. It's also not a good idea to keep it in a brokerage account, because the market has cyclical ups and downs. Your emergency fund money should be accessible whenever you need it, so online savings is the best way to go, even though you earn next to nothing in these accounts.

Now, why do I say fund your retirement accounts *before* you fund your emergency account? Simple—if you truly have an emergency, you can usually either borrow against or withdraw the funds and escape a penalty.

On the other hand, if you skip funding your retirement for a few years until you build up your emergency savings, you're missing out on hundreds of thousands of dollars—a true retirement emergency.

For most people, emergencies are rare. Even if you *do* pay a 10% penalty to withdraw your retirement savings when you have one, you've had the benefit of compound growth for several years and a small penalty amount is insignificant in comparison.

STEP FIVE: INDEX FUNDS FOR OTHER GOALS

I don't endorse the idea of a house fund, a vacation fund, a savings fund—I think you should focus on *building wealth* and then the money will be there whenever you need it.

Here's what I mean: if you're consistently putting money in your brokerage account and buying index funds, you're building wealth you can use for whatever you want, whenever you need it. If you have medium- to long-range goals for your money, there's no better place to put it.

Now, you do have to be smart and not risk money you're counting on in the short term. If you're saving for a house, it's fine to keep your money in index funds until you're within a year or two of buying. At that point, you should move it to a cash account or fixed-income fund. You don't want to be the guy who loses 10% of his down payment in a market correction a week before closing.

WHAT ABOUT COLLEGE SAVINGS?

In the card game of life, your retirement trumps your kids' college...every time. If you can't pay for your kids' education, they can take out loans. There are no retirement loans —*you are on your own*. And I'm sure if you asked your kids if they'd rather make student loan payments for five or 10 years, or help you out in retirement for 20 or 30, they'd take the student loan payments...every time.

If you really want to save for college, go ahead—after you fully fund your retirement. If you have money left over, then by all means, put it in index funds to help cover tuition. If you're consistently building wealth during your working years, there will be money in your brokerage account for college.

A WORD ABOUT 529 PLANS

These are gaining traction as college savings plans, and if you have extra money to save, they may make sense for your family. While contributions are not tax-deductible for federal income tax purposes, most states offer state tax incentives. If you live in California, Delaware, Hawaii, Kentucky, Massachusetts, Minnesota, New Hampshire, New Jersey, North Carolina, or Tennessee, however, you don't get a state tax deduction.

Your money grows tax-free in a 529 plan and withdrawals are not taxed as long as you use them for qualified education expenses.

Money in	Taxed
Money grows	Not taxed
Money out	Not taxed

You can use the money in your 529 plan for tuition, room, board, books, supplies, and equipment at any vocational school, four-year college, graduate school, and even private K-12 institutions. State 529 plans aren't limited to your children, either. You can open one for yourself or even your grandchildren, if you want.

If you do decide to go the 529 route, shop different state plans to see what funds are available and what they charge in expenses. One nice thing about 529 plans is that you can live in one state, invest in another state's 529 plan, and use the money for college in a different state.

You can save for college if you really want to, but you should always prioritize your own retirement savings before you funnel money into a 529 plan. Remember, your kids can get loans—and if you're in a position to do so, you can offer to help repay them after they graduate.

Why can't I just take educational withdrawals from my IRA?

Technically, you can, because there is no 10% penalty for educational expenses. But again, I don't recommend raiding your retirement to pay your kids' college bills. Unless you're so far ahead of your retirement savings goals that running out of money isn't a possibility, your number-one priority is your IRA and 401(k).

Remember, if your kids really want to go to college, they have many options to pay for it. Your options for covering your expenses in retirement are limited to what you manage to save.

KEY TAKEAWAYS

- Paying for retirement is your number-one savings priority.
- You should always fund your 401(k) up to the company match. Whether you max it out depends on your fund options.
- A traditional IRA is always the best choice if you qualify; only fund a Roth IRA if you can't get a tax deduction contributing to another account.
- Saving for retirement is more important than saving for college. Only fund a college plan *after* you've fully funded your retirement accounts. Your kids can get student loans, but there are no government loans for retirement.

CHAPTER 9

OTHER RETIREMENT INCOME AND ASSETS

You've probably noticed that we spent a lot of time talking about things you should be doing to save for retirement—the accounts you should open, the funds you should buy, and how to structure your retirement savings. But we haven't spent much time talking about retirement cash you *don't* necessarily have much control over.

In this chapter, I'm going to focus on things like Social Security and pensions that aren't under your control. I'm also going to touch on using your home as a retirement asset and whether that's a good idea. Finally, I'll touch on annuities and why they don't make sense for most people.

These things can all be part of your overall retirement plan, but as I'll show you, they shouldn't be foundational. If you're relying on them for retirement security, you may be sorely disappointed.

WHAT EXACTLY IS SOCIAL SECURITY?

Social Security is retirement income paid by the federal government. It's funded by payroll deductions—those FICA taxes taken from your check every month. If you draw a paycheck, you pay 7.65% for Social Security and Medicare and your employer pays the same. If you're self-employed, you pay the whole 15.3% yourself.

Everyone who pays FICA taxes for at least 10 years—or is married to someone who has paid them—is eligible for Social Security. If you're a stay-at-home parent or one who only worked part-time for a few years, you can draw up to 50% of your spouse's Social Security benefit.

Now, if you're a trust-funder, you're out of luck. But then again, if you're a trust-funder, you probably don't care.

HOW MUCH WILL YOU GET?

The truthful answer at this point is "who knows" because Social Security is a government program, and that means it can be changed—and likely will be—in the future. It's gone through significant evolutions since President Roosevelt signed it into law in 1935. Most recently, the 1983 amendments increased the Social Security tax to its current 15.3% and raised the retirement age to 67 to keep the program solvent into the 21st century.

If you follow the news, you know Social Security is a hot-button issue. It's generally understood that the program is running out of money and benefits will have to be reduced sometime around 2034 unless Congress acts to amend the program again.

That said, it's highly unlikely Social Security will ever *go away*. It is likely, however, that the retirement age will be raised again, the payroll tax will be expanded, and/or the benefit formula recalculated. Most people will retire with some form of Social Security, it's just impossible to predict what it will look like 20 years from now.

Social Security benefits are currently calculated with a complex formula that takes into account the number of years you worked, your salary and contributions during those years, and the age you are when you take retirement benefits. If you only worked 10 or 15 years, or severely under-reported your self-employed income, your benefit will be much lower than a high-earning executive with 40 years in the workforce.

In 2019, the maximum monthly benefit for a 62-year-old, the youngest age you can be and still draw benefits, is $2,209. The maximum benefit for someone retiring at age 65 is $2,757, and the maximum monthly benefit for someone who takes his first benefit check at age 70 or over is $3,770. The vast majority of people getting Social Security in 2019 receive between $800 and $1,800 a month.

Chetna owned a small fro-yo shop for 25 years. She paid her self-employed payroll tax every year on her business profit, but she used every legal deduction in the book to lower her taxable income. Although the shop turned a profit of nearly $100,000 every year, Chetna only paid FICA on about $60,000. When she retired at 65, her Social Security benefit was only about $1,700 a month.

Richard spent 30 years in R&D for a petrochemical company. For the last 10 years of his career, his salary was above the Social Security tax cut-off. As a result, he qualified for the maximum benefit. He was anxious to retire after so many years in a demanding, high-stress job, so he elected to retire and start taking his $2,209 monthly benefit as soon as he turned 62.

Martha was a stay-at-home mom until her late 40s, when her twins started college and her husband divorced her in the middle of his midlife crisis. She had no choice but to return to work as a nurse at the university hospital. Although she had worked over 10 years and qualified for Social Security when she turned 62, she elected to work part-time a few more years and delay collecting benefits until she turned 70 so she could get a larger check.

WHEN SHOULD I TAKE SOCIAL SECURITY BENEFITS?

Although the age for full retirement benefits has increased to 67, you can still elect to draw checks at age 62. You get the maximum amount if you delay benefits until age 70.

For planning purposes, I recommend using the benefit you're entitled to at age 62. It's best to be conservative with Social Security benefits when you're calculating what you need in retirement savings to meet your income needs.

And if you're in a position financially to retire at 62 and collect Social Security, it's actually not a bad idea, especially if you don't need it to meet your living expenses. But you do need to keep in mind that your benefits will be reduced if you have earned income beyond a certain amount (about $17,000 in 2019) and take Social Security early. Once you reach full retirement age, earned income won't decrease your benefits.

If you can invest your Social Security checks in index funds until you reach age 70, you'll have enough in your account to cover about 16 years of difference between the maximum payment at age 62 and the maximum payment at age 70. For me? I'd rather have the money to use or invest my way *now* than wait 8 years for a slightly larger payment.

Bari qualified for the maximum Social Security benefit and elected to take her retirement checks at age 62. She invested the $2,209 each month in index funds and continued to work a couple months a year as a consultant. At age 70, she had $300,000 in the index fund account in addition to her IRA and 401(k). She continued drawing her $2,209 a month until her death at 82. In total, her Social Security benefits netted her $300,000 for the first eight years and $318,000 in the final 12 years of her life, for a total of $618,000.

Walt also qualified for the maximum Social Security benefit, but he elected to postpone benefits until age 70, when he drew $3,770 a month. He also died at age 82, by which time he had received $543,000 in Social Security payments.

The Social Security bottom line: whatever you do, don't

over-rely on the role of Social Security to fund your lifestyle in retirement. It's impossible to know today what you might get when you're ready to retire.

I'm being brutally honest here: if you're counting on Social Security as a major part of your retirement income, you need to re-evaluate your savings plan.

WHAT ABOUT PENSIONS?

A pension is a defined benefits retirement plan. The employer guarantees you a certain income for life after you retire. In most cases, once you die, your benefits "die" with you; you can't leave your pension to your wife or children.

Most retirement plans are defined contribution plans, which means your employer puts a certain amount into your 401(k) plan each year you are employed. This money belongs to you once you are vested. If there's money in your account when you die, you can leave it to your heirs.

Unless you're in the public sector or belong to a union, you probably don't need to worry about pensions. About 77% of public sector workers have a pension plan; in the private sector, only about 13% will get pensions.

I'm not going to spend too much time on pensions because they vary wildly depending on the employer, the state, and years worked. If you have a pension, you know your numbers far better than I or anyone else ever will. In fact, most people I know with pensions know *to the day* when they can retire and what they will pocket every month once they do.

If you have a pension, by all means, plug it into your retirement savings calculator. Just remember, pension payments rarely keep up with inflation, so your "generous" retirement check at age 55 might not feel so generous when you are 75.

Sandra was a public school administrator for 30 years, eligible for retirement at 55 with a pension of $42,000. She had no children and she had paid off her condo three years ago. Between her IRA savings and pension, she felt she could safely retire at 55.

Things were great the first few years, although her cost of living raises were rarely above 1%. However, the year she turned 60, the state legislature approved a huge property tax increase. To make matters worse, her condo fees went up by $300 a month to cover major improvements. She had to increase her IRA distributions by $600 a month to cover the shortfall, so instead of having 25 years of supplemental income in her IRA, she now had just 12.

IF MY HOUSE IS PAID OFF, ISN'T THAT A RETIREMENT ASSET?

There's something appealing about owning your home and having no mortgage payments dragging you down. It's like free housing, not to mention the half-a-million dollars in real estate you own.

At least, that's the conventional wisdom.

The truth is a bit more complicated. The most obvious

issue is that a home isn't a liquid asset. You can't break off a piece to sell when you need money for living expenses. And if you want to talk about how real estate performs as an asset compared to index funds, it's not even close. Over the long haul, home prices have gained about 4% a year, which is half the rate of growth of the S&P 500.

Sure, you can get cash out of your house with a HELOC or a reverse mortgage, but you're going to pay the lender for the privilege, knocking your gains down even more.

Liquidity aside, owning a home does *not* equal free housing. Most homeowners spend between 2% and 4% of their home's value in upkeep and repairs each year. If you have a $500,000 house, that's between $10,000 and $20,000 a year just to keep your home in good order. If you have HOA or condo fees, you're spending even more.

In the end, you may come out ahead by selling your home, investing the proceeds, and renting something suitable. I'm not necessarily recommending that, but if you're counting on your home value for retirement, you should at least weigh all the costs.

————

Here's what I've learned over the years as an executor: people who have a large amount of their wealth in retirement tied up in a home usually don't have the cash flow to maintain it properly. The house falls into disrepair, and the only way they can get the money to fix it is to sell it—a catch-22. They don't want to sell it because it's the only asset they have to leave to their family. The house doesn't hold its value, and the heirs have to sell at a loss. It's far from an ideal situation.

On the other hand, if the home represents a small portion of their retirement assets, people usually have the money to maintain and improve it. The home gains value in retirement because it's well kept. In this case, it actually represents a solid asset in retirement.

If you're approaching retirement with more than half your wealth tied up in your home, you need to re-think holding onto it as your "free housing" option.

WHAT ABOUT ANNUITIES?

To the uninformed, annuities sound like a great idea. They promise guaranteed income later in exchange for payments now.

The reality is quite a bit different from the promise, however. Annuities are *not* investments; they're more like insurance contracts. They lock you and the insurance company into an agreement, and if you try to get out of it, the surrender fees are enormous.

In addition, you pay commissions, usually between 1% and 10%, which are built into the contract, so you don't see exactly what you're paying each year. They're very complicated instruments—intentionally so.

When you pay premiums to an insurance company for an annuity, some of your money is invested, some goes to commissions and other fees, and some goes to the insurance company to offset the risk involved in guaranteeing your income. The rate of return is pretty terrible.

Don't forget, an annuity is only as good as the company selling it—and there is no federal insurance program like the FDIC covering annuities. Annuities don't make sense for the vast majority of people.

KEY TAKEAWAYS

- Social Security *probably* isn't going anywhere, but it's impossible to predict what it will look like when you retire. Be conservative in your estimates for retirement planning purposes.
- Waiting to collect benefits until you're 70 sounds like a good idea until you do the math. I always prefer money in the bank *today* over a promise of something more 8 years from now.
- A pension is great if you have one, but don't count on it keeping up with inflation.
- If your home is a small part of your overall retirement wealth, it's not a bad idea to consider keeping it as part of your estate. If it represents a majority of your wealth, you should consider selling at retirement.

CHAPTER 10

HOW MUCH TO SAVE FOR RETIREMENT

By this point, you probably realize how important it is to save for retirement—it should be your first financial priority. But we haven't really talked about *how much* you should be setting aside.

In this chapter, we'll talk about a few of the more popular "rule of thumb" approaches to retirement savings. I don't necessarily recommend one approach over another, but I do suggest you run the numbers for each based on your financial situation to find the one that makes sense for you.

A word of caution about retirement savings—it *is* possible to go overboard. Here's what I mean by that: some people get so obsessed with amassing a retirement fortune, they forget to enjoy their lives *in the moment.* There's nothing wrong with amassing a retirement fortune, unless it deprives you of all pleasure while you're doing it.

It's all about finding the right balance. Save diligently to accumulate enough to live comfortably in retirement, but leave yourself enough cash to live comfortably *today,* too.

FOUR FORMULAS FOR RETIREMENT SAVINGS

Depending on who you ask, you'll probably get one of these rule-of-thumb formulas to help you estimate how much you should have invested by the time you retire. I'll explain how they work and give you the pros and cons of each.

Keep in mind, these formulas are based on the assumption that you've moved the bulk of your retirement savings to fixed-income funds by the time you retire. They don't take into account the additional growth you'll achieve if you keep your money in index funds even after you retire. Remember Warren Buffett's ideal allocation? If you follow my plan, your retirement money will be invested 90% in index funds and 10% in fixed assets—and it will stay there, making more money while you enjoy your retirement.

Desmond had $1.75 million in his IRA when he decided to retire. His financial advisor told him he could safely withdraw $70,000 a year in retirement based on his assets, which Desmond felt was more than enough combined with his Social Security. He promptly moved 75% of his money into fixed income assets and planned for a long and relaxing retirement knowing he wouldn't run out of money for 25 years.

Delilah only had $1 million in her retirement account when she decided to retire. She also planned to take $70,000 a year from her account, but unlike Desmond, she left her savings in index funds averaging 8% a year. Her account would support 32 years of $70,000 withdrawals.

THE 15% OF SALARY APPROACH

This school of thought recommends that you invest 15% of your gross salary—the money you earn before taxes and other deductions—in your retirement account. You can spread this between your 401(k) and IRA, but your total contributions should equal 15% of your earnings every year.

Michelle started saving for retirement when she got her first job after college. Her employer offered 6% matching funds for her 401(k), so Michelle put 6% of her $60,000 salary, or $3,600, into a growth fund in her 401(k). She put 9%, or $5,400, in index funds into her IRA.

She increased her contributions each time she got a raise so that her retirement savings always equaled 15% of her gross pay.

As far as savings rules of thumb go, this method is extremely simple; you only need to calculate 15% of your salary each year to determine your contributions.

The problem is that this method isn't very precise, and it doesn't establish an end-goal you can use to measure your progress. It also doesn't account for age and circumstances. If you're 25 and just getting started, 15% will put you in a great position at retirement. On the other hand, if you're 40 and haven't prioritized retirement savings, 15% may not be nearly enough.

THE 1, 3, 5, 8 APPROACH

This is less a rule of thumb than a benchmark. The 1, 3, 5, 8 rule says that you should have a certain multiple of your annual salary in retirement savings at different age milestones. Fidelity uses this rule of thumb to give investors concrete savings goals. Here's how it works:

- By age 30, you should have **1** full year's salary in your retirement account
- By age 40, you should have **3** years' salary saved in your account
- By age 50, you should have **5** years' salary saved
- By age 60, you should have **8** years' salary saved

Fidelity tacks on one last target: by age 67, you need 10 times your salary in your retirement account.

By the time Garrett turned 30, his salary at the bank was $80,000. Because he'd only been working four years by then, his retirement account balance was just $48,000. He increased his 401(k) contributions to the max and opened an IRA, which he fully funded each year.

When Garrett turned 40, his diligence paid off and he had $355,000 in his retirement accounts. Even though his salary had increased to $105,000 over the past 10 years, he was actually slightly over his target of three times his salary, or $315,000.

On his 50th birthday, Garrett had $950,000 in his retirement account. He had been promoted to senior vice president the year before and his salary had increased to $175,000. He was over $100,000 ahead of his goal of five years' salary.

Garrett was eyeing retirement as he approached his 60th birthday, so he checked his account balance and did the math. Based on his current salary of $225,000, he would need at least $1.8 million in retirement savings. Since he had $2.2 million in his account, he was confident he could retire in the next year or two.

Although the 1, 3, 5, 8 approach doesn't tell you exactly how much to save for retirement, it does give you a simple way to benchmark your progress so you can make adjustments if you are too far behind or ahead.

The drawback is that it does nothing to help you reach your benchmarks. It's on you to figure out how much you should be saving each year. Even worse, because there is a 10-year interval between benchmarks, you won't be able to quickly adjust if you're falling behind.

You could underfund your retirement for 10 years without knowing it, depriving you of a full decade of compound growth on the extra contributions you should have made.

THE 4% RULE

The 4% rule says that you should be able to live for a full year on 4% of your retirement savings. This rule, like many others, is based on a 25-year life expectancy after retirement, which is where the 4% comes from: 4% per year multiplied by 25 years equals 100% of your retirement account.

Ginger and her husband Jack were aggressive savers throughout their careers; they planned to retire at 58 so they could travel while they were still relatively young and healthy. They figured they'd need $125,000 a year to support their anticipated lifestyle in retirement.

Using the 4% rule, Ginger and Jack needed $3 million in order to comfortably retire. Fortunately, their focus on retirement savings paid off and they had about $2.75 million in their IRAs. Since they planned to leave the bulk of their savings in index funds, they knew they had more than enough to last for 30 years.

This is another simple rule of thumb; it's easy to calculate how much you need in your retirement account to support your lifestyle.

On the downside, the 4% rule only works if you are earning at least 5% on your retirement savings to cover taxes and inflation—and if you are honest about how much you actually need to maintain your standard of living when you're retired. It's all too easy to convince yourself you can make do on half your current income if your account balance isn't where it should be.

Khalid was sick to death of his job after 30 years and counted down the days until he could retire. After a particularly brutal week, he decided to check the balance in his retirement account to see if he had enough to quit his job.

Khalid had $1.3 million in his 401(k). Using the 4% rule, he could withdraw $52,000 a year. Although his current salary was over $100,000, he almost convinced himself he could easily live on $52,000 a year if he tightened his belt.

Fortunately, when he got home that evening, his wife convinced him it would be impossible to maintain anything even close to their current lifestyle with such a huge cut in income. Khalid grudgingly agreed that he should work a few more years and make catch-up contributions to his IRA before walking away from his job.

THE "MAGIC RETIREMENT NUMBER" RULE

This rule assumes you'll need 80% of your income just prior to retirement to live comfortably after you leave work. It also assumes a 25-year life expectancy once you retire.

To find your magic number, you multiply 80% of your current income by 25 years. That's the amount you'll need in retirement savings before you retire. It's basically the 4% rule in reverse with a twist. Instead of looking at your account balance and deciding if you can live on 4% of it, you're starting with a yearly withdrawal amount and setting a goal for 25 years of income.

Tillie's salary was $130,000 the year before she planned to retire; her magic number was $2.6 million. To her dismay, she only had $1.9 million in her retirement account, which would only support $76,000 a year in distributions, well below the $104,000 a year she would need according to the magic number rule.

On the plus side, it's easy to calculate your magic number, and if you achieve it, it promises a comfortable lifestyle in retirement. But this method can be a bit discouraging because the savings goal is so aggressive.

But be aware that the magic number rule is a one-size-fits-all approach to retirement savings. Many people won't need fully 80% of their current income in retirement. You no longer have costs related to work such as commuting, dry cleaning, and eating out. Your income tax bracket typically goes down, so you pay less in taxes. Your house may be paid off and you likely won't carry as much debt—and you're probably not supporting and educating children.

In other words, you may only need 65% or 70% of your current income to maintain your lifestyle in retirement.

On the other hand, if you're someone who scrimped and

saved during your working years in order to live large in retirement, you may need 110% of your current salary in retirement.

If you're using the magic number formula, it's best to create a realistic retirement budget and see how it compares to your current salary. If your retirement budget represents 72% of your income, use that number instead of 80% to calculate your magic number.

KEY TAKEAWAYS

- Saving for retirement should be your number one financial priority—but don't get so goal-oriented that you can't enjoy your life along the way.
- There's no one-size-fits-all formula for retirement savings. Most of them simply serve as benchmarks to help you gauge your progress.
- Most rule-of-thumb approaches assume you're moving your savings to low-return, fixed income assets. If you keep your money in index funds, it will last much longer.
- No matter which method you use, it's a good idea to review your account balances each year and make adjustments to keep you on track.

CHAPTER 11

NEXT STEPS

THAT'S IT! MUCH SIMPLER THAN YOU THOUGHT, YES? Just leverage time, compounding, and low-cost index funds, and resist the pitches that tell you otherwise.

I'd love to hear your thoughts and experiences. Email me at retire@anthonyspark.com with any questions or if you start to feel pressured to hire a financial advisor. I'll help you stay on course.

GLOSSARY

401(k) — A 401(k) plan is a qualified retirement plan allowing eligible employees to save and invest for retirement using pre-tax dollars. You are limited to the investment choices offered by your plan.

Actively managed fund — An actively managed fund is a fund in which a management team chooses which stocks, bonds, or other assets to buy. Most funds are pegged to a benchmark index—actively managed funds usually aim to beat their benchmark (but usually fail).

Annuity — An annuity is a contract between you and an insurance company in which you pay premiums and the company pays you a guaranteed amount on a fixed schedule for a period of years or until you die. Annuities are like pensions you buy for yourself, except they're ridiculously expensive.

Asset allocation — Asset allocation is a strategy for dividing your investments into different asset classes (stocks, bonds, cash, etc.) in order to control your portfolio risk.

Bonds — A bond is basically an IOU from a government or corporation that pays you a fixed amount at regular intervals for a predetermined period of time.

Brokerage account — A brokerage account is a taxable account you open with a licensed broker who executes trades on your behalf.

Cash — Cash refers to liquid assets such as checking and savings accounts you can access immediately for full face value.

Certificates of deposit (CDs) — These are federally insured savings accounts that pay a fixed amount of interest on a fixed date. You pay a penalty if you cash them in before the withdrawal date. You can buy short-term CDs that mature in 12 months or less, or long-term CDs with terms of up to five years.

Commission — This is a fee charged by your broker when you buy or sell a security. They are also called transaction fees or trading fees.

Compound growth — Compound growth is "earnings on earnings." A $1,000 investment at 10% earns $100 in year one. In year two, earnings are paid on $1,100 (the original $1,000 plus $100 in earnings).

Contributions — This is money you contribute to an IRA or 401(k) in order to save for retirement. There are annual contribution limits for each type of account. Some contributions are tax deductible.

Distributions — Distribution is the word the IRS applies to retirement account withdrawals. You may owe income tax on your distributions, depending on the type of account you withdraw the money from.

Early withdrawal penalty — If you take money from a qualified retirement account (IRAs, 401(k) plans) before age 59-½, you may owe a penalty in addition to income tax on the money you withdraw. In some cases, the penalty is waived, although the taxes aren't.

Earned income — Earned income is money you get from paid work (hourly, salary, contract, etc.). Income from a trust, unemployment payments, worker's compensation, pensions, and Social Security are not considered earned income.

Employer match — Many employers incentivize retirement savings by offering a dollar-for-dollar 401(k) contribution on your behalf up to a certain percentage of your salary. If your employer match is 5%, your employer matches your contributions up to 5% of your salary. This money is not reported as income.

Exchange traded fund (ETF) — An ETF is like a mutual fund, except it is traded on a stock exchange just like a stock. ETFs can hold virtually any type of assets, including stocks, bonds, commodities, currencies, and even cryptocurrency.

Expense ratio — The expense ratio is the amount, expressed as a percentage, that the company charges to operate a mutual fund. It includes administrative expenses and management fees. If the expense ratio is 0.40%, you pay $40 a year on a $10,000 investment.

Fee-only financial planner — A fee-only financial planner charges you an hourly rate or a set amount for planning and advice. Most financial planners charge a percentage of assets under management to manage your money.

FICA tax — FICA is a mandatory payroll tax that funds Medicare and Social Security. The FICA tax rate is 15.3%, which is equally split between employers and employees. If you are self-employed, you pay the full 15.3% yourself.

Fixed income fund — Fixed income assets, typically bonds, pay a fixed return on a regular schedule. A fixed income fund holds bonds and other fixed income assets. These are rock-solid investments, but they pay tiny returns. Fixed income funds are generally the safest funds.

Gross pay — This is your actual salary before any deductions are taken out for taxes, insurance, retirement, etc.

Index fund — An index fund is a type of mutual fund pegged to a stock index. The fund manager buys the same stocks in the same proportion as the underlying index and seeks to replicate, not beat, the returns of that index.

Inflation — Inflation is the rate of increase in the cost of goods and services and the corresponding loss of your currency's purchasing power.

Management fees — This is the fee charged by a fund manager to invest capital on behalf of investors. Management fees are included in the total expense ratio.

Mutual fund — A mutual fund is a pool of money contributed by many different investors that is invested in stocks, bonds, or other assets. A mutual fund share represents a tiny fraction of the total assets held by the fund.

Net pay — This is the money you take home after deductions. Your net pay is the amount that shows up in your checking account on payday.

Online brokerage — An online brokerage is a licensed brokerage that operates over the internet instead of face-to-face. Popular online brokers include TD Ameritrade and E*Trade. Many investment firms also offer online brokerage accounts including Vanguard, Fidelity, and Charles Schwab.

Online savings accounts — Online savings accounts are just like savings accounts offered by a brick-and-mortar bank, except there are no branches. Because of the low overhead, most online savings accounts pay higher interest rates.

Passively managed fund — This is another term for an index fund. It's the opposite of an actively managed fund, because the fund manager isn't picking stocks and trying to beat the market. The fund manager's role is simply to replicate the holdings of the underlying stock index.

Pension — A pension is a defined benefit plan provided by an employer or union. When you retire, you are guaranteed a fixed amount of income each year until you die. Pensions aren't owned assets like IRAs and 401(k) plans; they can't be passed down to heirs after you die.

Portfolio — Your portfolio is all your saved and invested assets. You may have stocks, mutual funds, bonds, cash and cash equivalents, and even real estate in your portfolio.

Pre-tax — Pre-tax money is money that comes off your reportable income for tax purposes. If you make $10,000 in pre-tax contributions to your 401(k), your reported income goes down by $10,000.

Rebalance — Rebalancing is the act of periodically buying and selling assets in your portfolio to bring it into alignment with your desired asset allocation. For example, if your preferred asset allocation is 90% index funds and 10% bonds and you had $500,000 in your portfolio, $450,000 would be in funds and $50,000 in bonds. At the end of the year, your funds will likely have earned much more than your bonds, so your portfolio might have $500,000 in index funds and $51,000 in bonds. To get back to a 90/10 asset allocation, you would rebalance your portfolio by selling $4,000 worth of funds and buying an equivalent amount in bonds.

Required Minimum Distribution (RMD) — This is the amount of money you are required to withdraw from your retirement accounts each year to avoid a penalty. RMDs typically start on April 1st in the year after you turn 70-½. The amount depends on your age, account balance, and beneficiaries. If you don't take your RMDs, you pay a penalty equal to 50% of the amount you should have taken.

Roth IRAs are not subject to RMDs while the owner is alive.

Returns — This is another word for earnings. If a fund returns 8% a year, it means you earn 8% on the money you have invested.

Risk tolerance — This is the amount of market volatility you can stand before you lose your mind and sell off shares in a panic. Most funds generally indicate a risk level in the prospectus; low-risk funds typically have lower returns.

Robo-advisor — A robo-advisor replaces a human advisor with a computer algorithm. You pay a management fee to a robo-advisor and in exchange, it invests your money into a preset portfolio of assets based on your age, income, and risk level.

Roth IRA — A Roth IRA is a qualified retirement account. You make contributions with after-tax dollars, but withdrawals are tax-free. If you contribute to a Roth, you don't get to take a deduction on your tax return. If you are in a very low tax bracket, a Roth IRA may make more sense than a traditional IRA. If you think you will be in a lower tax bracket when you retire, you lose money with a Roth. All IRAs have annual contribution limits.

Self-employed 401(k) — A self-employed 401(k) is a retirement savings vehicle for business owners who have no employees other than the owner and/or a spouse. The business owner can make contributions both as an individual employee and as a business/employer, which maximizes retirement savings and business deductions.

Self-employment tax — This is another word for FICA taxes paid by self-employed people. If you are self-employed, you pay the full 15.3%, but you get to deduct half on your tax return.

SEP IRA — A Simplified Employee Pension IRA is a retirement plan with flexible contributions for self-employed people and small business owners.

SIMPLE IRA — SIMPLE IRAs are for small businesses and allow for both employee and employer contributions. It has lower contribution limits than other small business IRAs.

S&P 500 — The S&P (or Standard and Poor's) 500 is a market-capitalization-weighted index of the 500 largest U.S. publicly traded companies. It's considered a good indicator of the U.S. economy and stock market as a whole.

Stock — A stock is a share of ownership in a company. When a company grows and becomes more valuable, the price of each individual share goes up. Some stocks pay dividends, or a percentage of the company's profits, on a quarterly basis, but they have no fixed interest rate or guarantees. Stocks are also called equities.

Stock index — A stock index tracks the performance of the stock market, or a specific portion of it. It also serves as a benchmark to measure the returns of other investments. Indices usually use a weighted formula, so larger companies count more in the calculation. In the S&P 500, for example, Apple is just one company, but it accounts for 2.9% of the index.

Target date fund — Target date funds are a type of mutual fund that holds a mix of stocks, bonds, and other assets. These funds are designed so that your asset allocation gradually changes to a more conservative mix as you approach retirement (your target date). They typically follow a formula that shifts the majority of your money away from stocks and into bonds and fixed income assets the closer you get to age 65.

Taxable income — Not to be confused with net pay, your taxable income is the money you actually pay taxes on after all allowable exemptions and deductions, such as mortgage interest, are subtracted. This is also known as adjusted gross income, or AGI. It includes both earned and unearned income.

Tax-advantaged — This is a blanket phrase used to describe any investment or account that is either tax-exempt, tax-deferred, or subject to other special tax treatment.

Tax shelter — A tax shelter is any investment or account that lets you stash cash to reduce your taxable income.

Traditional IRA — A traditional IRA is a retirement account where you contribute money with pre-tax dollars and pay taxes on money you withdraw in retirement. There are annual contribution limits, and you are required to take distributions the year after you turn 70-½. Since most people are in a lower tax bracket in retirement than they are during their working years, a traditional IRA is the smarter move for retirement savings.

Transaction costs — These are fees you pay for buying and

selling investments in a brokerage account. They are also known as commissions or trading fees.

Treasuries (notes, bills, bonds) — Treasuries collectively describe any debt instruments issued by the federal government. They have fixed interest rates and fixed terms that can be as short as four weeks or as long as 30 years. These are considered risk-free assets and thus have pitifully small rates of return.

Wimpy — A character in the Popeye comic who understood the time value of money, especially as it applies to hamburgers.

IF YOU LIKED THIS BOOK...

Thanks for reading! If you enjoyed this book, I'd appreciate your honest review on Amazon, BookBub, GoodReads, or your favorite store.

And please join my email list for new book announcements: https://anthonyspark.com/join

ABOUT THE AUTHOR

Anthony S. Park is host of the popular podcast *Simple Money Wins* (available on YouTube, iTunes, and anthonys-park.com).

He is a New York executor, attorney, and entrepreneur. Anthony's cases have been featured in many places, including the *Wall Street Journal*, *New York Times*, CNBC, and *MarketWatch*.

How to Buy Your Perfect First Home: What Every First-Time Homebuyer Needs to Know

How Probate Works: A Guide for Executors, Heirs, and Families

How to Hire an Executor: For Your Loved One's Estate or Your Will

How to Get Promoted: Simple Steps to Better Title and Higher Pay

INDEX

N

Nasdaq Composite Index, 23

net asset value, 61

net pay

    defined, 119

90/10 example, 50–51

O

1, 3, 5, 8 approach, 106–107

online brokerage, 83

    defined, 119

online calculators, 79

online savings accounts

    defined, 119

P

passively managed fund

    defined, 119

pensions, 77, 98–99

    defined, 119–120

self-employment, 74–76

self-employment tax

defined, 122

SEP IRA (Simplified Employee Pension IRA), 75

defined, 122

short-term bonds, 47

short-term notes, 76

SIMPLE IRAs, 75

defined, 122

60/40 Example, 50

social security, 4, 94–98

tax, 77

S&P (or Standard and Poor's) 500, 10–11, 17, 19, 23, 29, 30, 39, 41–42, 55

defined, 122

S&P 500 index funds, 22, 24–27, 31, 32, 37, 48, 50, 77, 82

SPIVA (S&P Indices Versus Active) Scorecard, 27, 29, 39

stock

defined, 122

Printed in Great Britain
by Amazon

10993627R00088